D1554957

Readings
In
Classical
Ethics

Edited by
John C. Wilhelmsson

Chaos To Order Publishing
San Jose, California

CONTENTS

DEDICATION

For all those who have believed in me and encouraged me despite any bad reports. My success stands upon your kindness.

And to all those who continue to allow me to practice the art of teaching.

READINGS IN CLASSICAL ETHICS

INTRODUCTION

The thought at the heart of this current work is that a reader should be something one can easily read. Having developed a pedagogy of direct readings from the classic philosophers in all of my ethics courses the small font and large number of selections in other readers was beginning to become a problem. "Readings In Classical Ethics" corrects these issues by offering both large print and a small number of classic selections.

"Classic" can of course have at least two different meanings. With selections on Plato, Aristotle, Epicurus, Seneca, and Augustine the classical period of philosophy is certainly well represented. And with John Dewey's "The Hebrew Moral Development" and Miles Dawson's "The Ethics Of Confucius" both "classic" western and eastern religious ethics are also covered. With more recent ethical "classics" such as Kant's "Groundwork of the Metaphysics of Morals" and J.S. Mill's "Utilitarianism" also being featured.

With diversity being such an important current topic "Readings In Classical Ethics" offers a positive argument for diversity from the classical world itself in the form of Augustine's "The Happy Life." It also models diversity by featuring selections from both men and women, and eastern and western thought.

However, "Readings In Classical Ethics" does more than just look back. For in the Edith Stein selection the philosophy of phenomenology presents an important new methodology for doing ethics. Her clear understanding of empathy, and the feminism that arises out of it, continues to have great promise as a building block of future ethical theory. Another important new perspective on ethics is featured in the selection "A Care Approach" by Rita Manning. Thus "Readings in Classical Ethics" both begins and ends with a feminine perspective.

This reader is based upon my belief that students should be, as much as is possible, directly exposed to the thought of history's great ethical thinkers so that they might develop their own ability to understand and apply ethical theory. Future ethical situations may be novel, yet those with a strong grasp of theory will always be well equipped to act. Thus the classic ethical question of "How can I live the good and happy life?" is still one very much worth pursuing today.

THE TRANSPOSITION OF EDITH STEIN
by John C. Wilhelmsson

Definition and Method

Edmund Husserl often had his doctoral students review the thought of another thinker on the same topic as their own doctoral theme as a starting point for study. This is the process Edith Stein engage in so I propose we follow that same path. Yet let us first, for the sake of clarity, define the term "empathy" and give a basic explanation of the phenomenological reduction.

When discussing the question of a given person attempting to enter into the "feeling" of another person a controversy often arises between the use of the word "empathy" or "sympathy." Edith Stein seeks to put this question to rest promptly:

> *All these data of foreign experience point back to the basic nature of acts in which foreign experience is comprehended. We now want to designate these acts as empathy, regardless of all historical traditions attached to the word.*

The purpose here is to help the reader realize that the investigation being entered into has little to do with the common usage of the words "empathy" and "sympathy." These are terms we use to describe acts in which foreign experience is comprehended. However, the investigation we shall now enter into is concerned with the act itself: With the phenomenology of empathy.

The phenomenological reduction must first be understood. If I wish to intuit a given object, say a chair, I must first bracket off all of the things and facts I know about said object. I now enter into a state of pure consciousness as a subject which encounters an object by intending to it. However, this process of intentionality takes place only from a certain perspective, within a short moment in time. Therefore, I can only look upon the chair from a certain limited perspective which will only give the chair a certain limited meaning to me. Perhaps I see the chair directly from above so I am unaware of its legs. Then I intend to it from the side and become more aware of its features. Now by intending to it over and over again, thus seeing it from several different perspectives, I have the possibility of gaining determinate knowledge of the chair.

Are intending to objects, like a chair, and intending to another human person in an attempt to have empathy analogous to one another? Edith Stein speaks of seeing a friend who has just lost a loved one and becoming aware of that friend's pain. This awareness might come about as a result of a strained tone of voice or a pale and emotionless face. Yet, by intending to my friend's pain from many different perspectives can I come to have determinate knowledge of it? Stein states:

> *I can consider the expression of pain, more accurately, the change of face I empathically grasp as an expression of pain, from as many sides as I desire. Yet, in principle, I can never gain an "orientation" where the pain itself is primordially given.*

Both the chair and my friend are objects present to my senses in the here and now yet my perception of objects and empathy are of a different nature. For I have the possibility of gaining determinate knowledge about the chair, however, I can never have the possibility of gaining determinate knowledge about the pain of my friend. Perhaps through a series of many intentions from many different perspectives I might ideally come to know how the pain effects my friend as a physical object. Yet, I can never in any condition fully gain access to the subject of the pain itself.

Stein further delineates this basic difference in nature between attending to an object and seeking to have empathy for another person.

> *When it arises before me all at once, it faces me as an object (such as the sadness I "read in another's face"). But when I inquire into its implied tendencies (try to bring another's mood to clear giveness to myself), the content, having pulled me into it, is no longer really an object. I am now no longer turned to the content but to the object of it, am at the subject of the content in the original subject's place.*

Edith Stein sees this shifting of the subject as the basic difference between empathy and memory, expectation or fantasy. For in all these later states the subject has continuity with the person having the memory, expectation or fantasy. However, in empathy the subject I face is not my own. I have now entered into the realm of intersubjectivity.

Philosophy of Empathy

Stein begins by pointing out the distinction between the physical body and the living body. The physical body is an object we perceive, like many others, yet in a certain specific way. She states:

> *Every other object is given to me in an infinitely variable multiplicity of appearances and of changing positions, and there are also times when it is not given to me. But this one object (my physical body) is given to me in successive appearances only variable within very narrow limits. As long as I have my eyes open at all, it is continually there with steadfast obtrusiveness, always having the same tangible nearness as no other object has. It is always "here" while other objects are always "there."*

It would seem that Stein is referring here only to the sensory data of the physical body. For whenever I open my eyes or engage in self-touch my physical body remains present through this sensory data. Yet what if I close my eyes and stretch out my limbs inside of a decompression chamber? Even in this state, where I have no sensory data of my physical body at all, my sense of embodiment remains inescapably present. The fact that I know this body belongs to me can never be known by outer perception alone because outer perception would involve only interrupted streams of sensory data while my sense of embodiment remains constant. This constant sense of embodiment, given to me only outside of sensory data, is my "living body."

The living body is not given to me as a sensation or as a group of sensations, but rather as the focal point of all of my sensations. It thus has an entirely different nature than that of my physical body. Stein says of this:

> *All these entities from which my sensations arise are amalgamated into a unity, the unity of my living body, and they are themselves places in the living body.*

Through this Edith Stein begins to speak of the living body as having a "zero point of orientation" which she refers to as the "I." She presents the example of a foreign physical object which could approach my living body, and even appear to be closer to my "I" than one of the outer limbs of my living body (or the sense of embodiment of said outer limb). Is this foreign physical object now closer to my zero point of orientation than my own outer limb? Edith Stein answers:

The distance of the parts of my living body from me is completely incomparable with the distance of foreign physical bodies from me. The living body as a whole is at the zero point of orientation with all physical bodies outside of it. "Body space" [Leibraum] and "outer space" are completely different from each other.

The problem remaining here for Stein is that one's own physical body can be perceived with the senses just as foreign physical objects are. Therefore, from the standpoint of the senses, what separates the two?

Stein has been speaking strictly of a body at rest up until this point. Yet once a body is put into motion a further understanding of the relationship between the living body and the physical body becomes possible.

When I move one of my limbs, besides becoming bodily aware of my own movement, I have an outer visual or tactile perception of physical body movements to which the limb's changed appearances testify. As the bodily perceived and outwardly perceived limb are interpreted as the same, so there also arises an identical coincidence of the living and physical body's movement. This constant sense of fusion between the living body and the physical body is one which cannot be broken. For wherever my physical body goes my living body must follow in an almost perfect and "indissoluble" union.

In terms of the phenomenological reduction Edith Stein points out that no matter what standpoint one takes in order to gain a perspective on a given object the physical body and the living body remain in this always and indissoluble union:

Every step I take discloses a new bit of the world to me or I see the old one from a new side. In doing so I always take my living body along. Not only am I always "here" but also it is; the various "distance" of its parts from me are only variations within this "here."

Thus the living body and the physical body are both necessary for the phenomenological reduction.

Stein now seeks to delve more deeply into the relationship between the living body and the physical body through the foot "gone to sleep" example. She describes the foot "gone to sleep" as being beyond the realm of the living body because of its lack of sensation. Like a "foreign physical body that I cannot shake off." Yet when circulation returns and the foot "awakes" it once again becomes a part of the living body. Stein points out the implications of this toward understanding the living body.

> For *the living body is essentially constituted through sensations; sensations are the real constituents of consciousness and, as such, belong to the "I." Thus how could there be a living body not the body of an "I"!*

Thus the concepts of the living body, the physical body and the "I" are joined together.

Stein goes on to investigate the relationship between the living body and feelings. She points out that this relationship is somewhat similar to the phenomenon of fusion already discussed between the living body and the physical body. However, one could wish to express a cheerful feeling yet be simply too physically exhausted to do so. She refers to this as "the phenomenon of the reciprocal action of psychic and somatic experiences." By this she means that the psychic depends upon the somatic in order to understand experiences. The consciousness of the "I" is always body bound.

Feelings have another particular characteristic to them for Stein. They are never complete in themselves but always seek, even demand, bodily expression.

> *Feeling in its pure essence is not something complete in itself. As it were, it is loaded with an energy which must be unloaded.*

She goes on to point out some of the many different ways a person might express feelings with bodily expression being the most normative among them. And although the bodily expression of feeling can be faked, expressed only in terms of the physical body, the actual phenomenon of the expression of feeling is a rather definite process.

> *I not only feel how feeling is poured into expression and "unloaded" in it, but at the same time I have this expression given in bodily perception. The smile in which my pleasure is experientially externalized is at the same time given to me as a stretching of my lips.*

So while it is possible to simply stretch your lips without the accompanying feeling and sense of unloading of said feeling in expression, the actual phenomenon of the expression of a feeling is a much more complex and definite experience.

This leads Edith Stein into a discussion of the role of the will within the psycho-physical individual. She sees the will not just as a mechanism of choice isolated in itself but as always seeking to be connected to action in a similar way as feelings always seek to be connected to expression.

The will employs a psycho-physical mechanism to fulfill itself, to realize what is willed, just as feeling uses such a mechanism to realize its expression.

With the main difference here being that the existence of feelings is something a person has little control over while the will is a voluntarily controlled function.

However, this begs an important question which should not be passed over. Edith Stein now moves on to the question of whether the will is causally determined. If the choices we make now are really our own or just the result of a long line of causality which we no longer have any control over.

Action is always the creation of what is not. This process can be carried out in causal succession, but the initiation of the process, the true intervention of the will is not experienced as a causal but as a special effect.

Stein does believe that causality plays a certain role in carrying out the will but only in terms of it being a conditioning factor. Such as when I will my body to move but it is very tired. However, she maintains that "All these causal relationships are external to the essence of the will."

Stein now transitions to a study of the foreign individual. Yet she first sums up what we have learned so far about the psychophysical individual.

> *The psycho-physical individual as a whole belongs to the order of nature. The living body in contrast with the physical body is characterized by having fields of sensation, being located at the zero point of orientation of the spatial world, moving voluntarily and being constructed of moving organs, being the field of expression of the experiences of its "I" and the instrument of the "I's" will.*

Given all of this information the question arises. How is empathy toward the foreign individual possible?

Edith Stein starts with the example of the inner perception of the living body being "co-given" with the outer perception of the physical body within a given individual. This fusion between the living body and the physical body of the individual then allows him or her to observe the foreign individual's living body and physical body being given in this same way. Once this is understood one can transpose their living body onto the foreign physical body of the other and begin to form an "empathic representation" of it.

Thus the key to understanding empathy is contained within the individual. For once I understand the relationship between my living body and my physical body all I need to do to is act as if the foreign physical body is my own physical body through putting my living body into relationship with it (either through fantasy or representations of my own past experience). She speaks of seeing someone's hand pressing on a table. If I wish to understand the sensations of this hand I simply act as if the foreign physical hand is my own physical hand and, by either recalling a time my hand was pressing on a table or by engaging in a fantasy about a possible experience, enter into relationship with it. Edith Stein refers to this act as a "co-comprehension" between my living body and the foreign physical hand.

Edith Stein more explicitly defines this new term while summing up the nature of sensual empathy. Notice the key role that the relationship between the living body and the physical body plays:

The possibility of sensual empathy is warranted by the interpretation of our own living body as a physical body and our own physical body as a living body because of the fusion of outer and bodily perception. It is also warranted by the possibility of spatially altering this physical body, and finally by the possibility of modifying its real properties in fantasy while retaining its type.

Thus it is only through a proper understanding of the nature of our own body and sense of embodiment that empathy for the foreign individual might become possible.

<u>Feminism</u>

When Edith Stein speaks of "transposing" my living body onto the foreign physical body of the other she is alluding to her idea that the nature of the human person is this integral union between the living body and the physical body. Yet just what is the living body? From her descriptions we know it is the constant sense of embodiment given to me only outside of my sensory data. That it is my zero point of orientation or "I." And that it is something which exists in an almost perfect union with my physical body yet has no physical attributes of its own. What else can Edith Stein be speaking of here except something that is very much like a soul? Thus we see here in Edith Stein's philosophy a perfect underpinning for the theological idea of Pope John Paul II that the body is a manifestation of the soul.

While this is an interesting connection in a certain sense it is not all that surprising. For in fact many philosophers down through the ages have written about the nature of the body and the soul. Plato thought that the body was the prison of the soul. Aristotle thought that the body and the soul were a composite. One of the first philosophers to write of the body as really being of benefit to the soul was St. Thomas Aquinas.

Aquinas saw the human body as being of great help to the human soul in gaining knowledge. This is because he saw the soul in its pure state as having a limited intellect and thus not being able to come to a full knowledge of the world without the sensory data of the body. In this way for Aquinas the body and the soul are connected to one another and, certainly in an intellectual sense, the soul relies upon the body to become fully manifest.

Thus what is so novel about what Pope John Paul II is saying here is not the idea that the body is a manifestation of the soul. What is so novel here is the idea that the soul is of two complimentary types—masculine and feminine. In his catechism of November 21, 1979 John Paul II is quite clear and explicit about this when he says of man and woman:

> *They are two ways of "being a body" and at the same time a man, which complete each other. They are two complementary dimensions of self-consciousness and self-determination and, at the same time, two complementary ways of being conscious of the meaning of the body.*

Aquinas held to the common thirteenth century view, based upon Aristotelian biology, that women were inferior to men. While more could be said about his views on women one thing is certain: The thought of Aquinas is not a good place to go looking for the philosophical underpinnings for the views expressed here by Pope John Paul II on the complementarity between man and woman. However, Aquinas is not really to blame in this for Aristotelian biology was simply the accepted thought of the thirteenth century.

Even if one searches throughout all of the other centuries and the entire history of philosophical thought on the body and the soul one is hard pressed to find anything similar to the idea Pope John Paul II puts forth here. This idea that there are two complimentary types of the human soul, masculine and feminine, is in fact something quite unique and novel. Indeed, I know of no other philosopher who has, with any sense of depth, put forth such an idea —save one.

After her work as Edmund Husserl's assistant Edith Stein sought a university academic appointment of her own. Despite her obvious talents and fine contributions she was at this time denied that opportunity. Perhaps this was all in God's plan as soon after this she began to feel drawn to Christianity. Not just Christianity in general but the Catholic faith in particular. She had chanced to read the autobiography of St. Teresa of Avila while staying at a friend's house and became fascinated by the great Carmelite Saint. After her conversion in 1922 she wished to join the Carmelites but did not do so immediately out of concern for her devoutly Jewish mother Auguste's feelings.

What happened next was a great blessing for all concerned. For Edith Stein was offered a position in the Dominican School at Speyer. Both living and working with the sisters allowed her the opportunity to begin to reflect upon women's education. Being a phenomenologist her reflections were deep. And the fruit of these reflections is the remarkable, yet still largely misunderstood, feminism of Edith Stein.

The first unique aspect of Stein's feminism is its sources. For she holds that it is a theology of feminism which is at the same time a philosophy of feminism:

> *Rightly understood and employed, the theological and philosophical approaches are not in competition, rather, they complete and influence each other.*

Stein further says of her method:

> *The philosophizing mind is challenged to make the realities of faith as intelligible as possible.*

Edith Stein holds that the revelation of the Bible creates a framework for feminism. Yet this framework must be built upon by reason in order to understand the full truth about woman. The Genesis story reveals that:

> *God created man according to his own image; in the divine image he created him; male and female he created them.*

From this Stein infers a philosophical truth:

> *I am convinced that the species humanity embraces the double species man and woman, that the essence of a complete human being is characterized by this duality; and that the entire structure of the essence demonstrates the specific character.*

Here we have a philosophical statement suggesting that human beings are not just one but two species—man and woman. Stein is obviously not using the term "species" in the biological sense here, for part of the definition of a biological species is the ability to reproduce, but rather in a logical sense in order to denote a dramatic difference between man and woman. Yet just what is this difference?

At this point many people become confused about Stein's thought. They see that she is making a bold statement about the nature of man and woman yet do not see any basis for it. Some have even gone as far as to suggest that Edith Stein is making a statement here that, in a philosophical sense, she cannot back up. Here it is necessary to understand Edith Stein's feminist thought within the context of her philosophical thought as a whole. She offers us some hints to this when she states: "Her entire essence demonstrates the specific character" and then goes on to note:

> *There is a difference not only in bodily structure and in particular physiological functions, but also in the entire corporal life. The relationship of soul and body is different in man and woman.*

Given this text alone it does seem like Edith Stein is making a rather bold statement about the nature of man and woman which she cannot, in a philosophical sense, back up. However, if you consider her thought here in light of a prior understanding of her work on empathy and the philosophy of intersubjectivity, which I hope the reader of this book is now in a good position to do, a great deal of light can be shone upon it.

Edith Stein holds that empathy takes place when I transpose my living body onto the foreign physical body of the other. This presupposes the idea that the living body and the physical body are joined in an indissoluble union and that this union shades not only the understanding I have of my own world (subjectivity) but also the understanding I have of the world of others (intersubjectivity). Now let us add to this calculation the factor of whether I have either a male or female physical body. If the relationship of my living body and my physical body shades my entire understanding of self and others will not the factor of my physical body being either male or female then become an extremely important one? Absolutely yes!

So when Edith Stein states that "The relationship of soul and body is different in man and woman" she is not making a statement which she cannot support. For one can refer to her doctoral dissertation On The Problem Of Empathy and find a lucid philosophical framework for such a statement. For in Stein's philosophy of empathy we understand ourselves through the pairing of our living body with our physical body and we understand the other through the pairing of our living body with the foreign physical body of the other.

In light of having come to know Edith Stein's thought more fully we can see that when she states: "The relationship of the soul and body is different in man and woman" she means that a soul that is embodied in a female body will in fact become different in nature than a soul that is embodied in a male body. Thus this sense of embodiment as female is the key to understanding the feminist thought of Edith Stein.[i]

THE REPUBLIC
by Plato
II

For Glaucon, who is always the most pugnacious of men, was dissatisfied at Thrasymachus' retirement; he wanted to have the battle out. So he said to me: Socrates, do you wish really to persuade us, or only to seem to have persuaded us, that to be just is always better than to be unjust?

I should wish really to persuade you, I replied, if I could.

Then you certainly have not succeeded. Let me ask you now:—How would you arrange goods—are there not some which we welcome for their own sakes, and independently of their consequences, as, for example, harmless pleasures and enjoyments, which delight us at the time, although nothing follows from them?

I agree that there is such a class, I replied.

Is there not also a second class of goods, such as knowledge, sight, health, which are desirable not only in themselves, but also for their results?

Certainly, I said.

And would you not recognize a third class, such as gymnastic, and the care of the sick, and the physician's art; also the various ways of money-making—these do us good but we regard them as disagreeable; and no one would choose them for their own sakes, but only for the sake of some reward which flows from them?

There is, I said, a third class also. Why do you ask?

Because I want to know in which of these three classes you would place justice?

In the highest class, I replied,—among those goods which the one who wishes to be happy desires both for their own sake and for the sake of their results...

Setting aside their rewards and results, I want to know what they are in themselves, and how they inwardly work in the soul. If you please, then, I will revive the argument of Thrasymachus. And first I will speak of the nature and the origin of justice according to the common view of them. Second, I will show that those who practice justice do so unwillingly, as a necessity, but not as a good. And third, I will argue that there is reason in this view, for the life of the unjust is after all far better than the life of the just...

I have never yet heard the superiority of justice to injustice maintained by any one in a satisfactory way. I want to hear justice praised in respect of itself; then I shall be satisfied, and you are the person from whom I think that I am most likely to hear this; and therefore I will praise the unjust life to the utmost of my power, and my manner of speaking will indicate the manner in which I desire to hear you too praising justice and censuring injustice. Will you say whether you approve of my proposal?

Indeed I do; nor can I imagine any theme about which a sensible man would more wish to converse.

I am delighted, he said, to hear you say so, and shall begin by speaking of the nature and origin of justice.

Glaucon

They say that to do injustice is, by nature, good; to suffer injustice, evil; but that the evil is greater than the good. And so when men have both done and suffered injustice and have had experience of both, not being able to avoid the one and obtain the other, they think that they had better agree among themselves to have neither; hence there arise laws and mutual covenants; and that which is ordained by law is termed by them lawful and just. This they affirm to be the origin and nature of justice;—that it is a mean or compromise, between the best of all, which is to do injustice and not be punished, and the worst of all, which is to suffer injustice without the power of retaliation; and justice, being at a middle point between the two, is tolerated not as a good, but as the lesser evil, and honored by reason of the inability of men to do injustice. For no man who is worthy to be called a man would ever submit to such an agreement if he were able to resist; he would be mad if he did. Such is the received account, Socrates, of the nature and origin of justice.

Now that those who practice justice do so involuntarily and because they have not the power to be unjust will be best illustrated if we imagine something of this kind: having given both to the just and the unjust the power to do what they will, let us watch and see where desire will lead them; then we shall discover that the very act of both the just and the unjust man will be proceeding down the same road, following their own interest, which all deem to be their good, and are only diverted into the path of justice by compulsion.

The liberty which we are supposing may be most completely given to them in the form of such a power as is said to have been possessed by Gyges the ancestor of Croesus the Lydian. According to the tradition, Gyges was a shepherd in the service of the king of Lydia; there was a great storm, and an earthquake made an opening in the earth at the place where he was feeding his flock. Amazed at the sight, he descended into the opening, where, among other marvels, he beheld a hollow bronze horse, having a doorway, at which he stooping and looking in saw a large dead body, as appeared to him, more than human, and having nothing on but a gold ring; this he took from the finger of the dead body. Now the shepherds met together, according to custom, that they might send their monthly report about the flocks to the king; into their assembly he came having the ring on his finger, and as he was sitting among them he chanced to turn the head of the ring inside of his hand, when instantly he became invisible to the rest of the company and they began to speak of him as if he were no longer present. He was astonished at this, and again touching the ring he turned the head outwards and reappeared; he made several trials of the ring, and always with the same results that when he turned the head inwards he became invisible, and when he turned it outwards he reappeared. Then he plotted to be chosen one of the messengers who was to be sent to the king; where as soon as he arrived he seduced the queen, and with her help conspired against the king and slew him, and took the kingdom.

Suppose now that there were two such magic rings, and the just man put on one of them and the unjust man the other; no man can be imagined to be of such an iron nature that he would stand fast in justice. No man would keep his hands off what was not his own when he could safely take what he liked out of the market, or go into houses and lie with any one at his pleasure, or kill or release from prison whom he wished, and in all respects be like a god among men. Then the actions of the just would be as the actions of the unjust; they would both come at last to the same point. And this we may truly affirm to be a great proof that a man is just, not willingly or because he thinks that justice is any good to him individually, but only by compulsion, for wherever anyone thinks that he can be unjust, there he is unjust. For all men believe in their hearts that injustice is far more profitable to the individual than justice, and he who argues as I have been supposing, will say that they are right. If you could imagine any one obtaining this power of becoming invisible, and never doing any wrong or touching what was another's, he would be thought by onlookers to be a most wretched idiot, although they would praise him to one another's faces, and keep up appearances with one another for a fear that they too might suffer injustice.

Now, if we are to form a real judgment of the life of the just and unjust man, we must isolate them; there is no other way; and how is the isolation to be effected? I answer: Let the unjust man be entirely unjust, and the just man entirely just; nothing is to be taken away from either of them, and both are to be perfectly furnished for the work of their respective lives. First, let the unjust man be like any other masters of his craft; like the skillful pilot or physician, who knows intuitively his own powers and keeps within their limits, and who, if he fails at any point, is able to recover himself. So let the unjust man make his unjust attempts perfectly, and remain hidden if he means to be great in his injustice: for the highest reach of injustice is:

to be deemed just when you are not. Therefore I say that in the perfectly unjust man we must assume the most perfect injustice; there is to be nothing taken away, so we must allow him, while doing the most unjust acts, to have acquired the greatest reputation for justice. If he takes a false step he must be able to recover; he must be one who can speak with effect, if any of his deeds come to light, and who can force his way where force is required by his courage and strength, and be rich in money and friends.

And at his side let us place the just man in his nobleness and simplicity, wishing, as Aeschylus says, to be and not to seem good. There must be no seeming, for if he seems to be just he will be honored and rewarded, and then we shall not know whether he is just for the sake of justice itself or for the sake of honors and rewards; therefore, let him be clothed in justice only, and have no other covering; and he must be imagined in a state of life the opposite of the former. Let him be the best of men, yet let him be thought the worst; then he will be put to the test; and we shall see whether he will be affected by the fear of infamy and its consequences. And let him continue this way to the hour of death; being just and seeming to be unjust. When both have reached the uttermost extreme, the one of justice and the other of injustice, let judgment be given which of them is the most happy.

Socrates

Heavens! My dear Glaucon, I said, how energetically you polish them up for the decision, first one and then the other, as if they were two statues.

Glaucon

I do my best, he said. And now that we know what they are like and there is no difficulty in tracing out the sort of life which awaits each of them. This I will proceed to describe; but as you may think the description a little too coarse, I ask you to suppose, Socrates, that the words which follow are not mine.— Let me put them into the mouths of the eulogists of injustice: They will tell you that the just man who is thought unjust will be scourged, racked, bound—will have his eyes burnt out; and, at last, after suffering every kind of evil, will be crucified: Then he will understand that he ought to seem only, and not be, just...

The unjust is pursuing a reality; he does not live with a view to appearances—he wants to be really unjust and not to seem only... In the first place, he is thought just, and therefore bears rule over the city; he can marry whom he wills, and give in marriage to whom he wills; he can trade where he likes, and always to his own advantage, because he has no misgivings about injustice and at every contest, whether in public or private, he gets the better of his antagonists, and gains at their expense, and is rich, and out of his gains he can benefit his friends, and harm his enemies; moreover, he can offer sacrifices, and dedicate gifts to the gods abundantly and magnificently, and can honor the gods or any man whom he wants to honor in a far better style than the just, and therefore he is likely to be dearer than they are to the gods. And thus, Socrates, gods and men are said to unite in making the life of the unjust man better than the life of the just man.

<u>Socrates</u>

I was going to say something to Glaucon, when Adeimantus, his brother, asked: Socrates, you do not suppose that there is nothing more to be urged?

Why, what else is there? I answered.
The strongest point of all has not even been mentioned, he replied. Well, then, according to the proverb, 'Let brother help brother'—if he fails in any part do you assist him; although I must confess that Glaucon has already said quite enough to lay me in the dust, and take from me the power of helping justice.

<u>Adeimantus</u>

Nonsense, he replied. But let me add something more: There is another side to Glaucon's argument about the praise and censure of justice and injustice, which is equally required in order to bring out what I believe to be his meaning. Parents and tutors are always telling their sons and their wards that they are to be just; but why? Not for the sake of justice, but for the sake of reputation; in the hope of obtaining for him who is reputed just some of those offices, marriages, and the like which Glaucon has numbered among the advantages accruing to the unjust from the reputation of justice. More, however, is made of appearances by this class of persons than by the others; for they throw in the good opinion of the gods, and will tell you of a shower of benefits which the heavens, as they say, rain upon the pious; and this accords with the testimony of the noble Hesiod and Homer, the first of whom says, that the gods make oaks of the just...

The cause of all this, Socrates, was indicated by us at the beginning of the argument, when my brother and I told you how astonished we were to find that of all the professing eulogists of justice— beginning with the ancient heroes of whom memorial has been preserved to us, and ending with the men of our own time—no one has ever blamed injustice or praised justice except with a view to the glories, honors, and benefits which flow from them. No one has ever adequately described, either in verse or prose, the true essential nature of either of them abiding in the soul, and invisible to any human or divine eye; or shown that of all the things of a man's soul which he has within him, justice is the greatest good, and injustice the greatest evil...

But I speak in this vehement manner, as I must frankly confess to you, because I want to hear from you the opposite side; and I would ask you to show not only the superiority which justice has over injustice, but what effect they have on the possessor of each of them which makes the one to be good and the other evil. And please, as Glaucon requested of you, exclude the appeal to reputations; for unless you take away from each of them his true reputation and add on the false, we shall say that you do not praise justice, but the appearance of it; we shall think that you are only exhorting us to keep injustice dark, and that you really agree with Thrasymachus in thinking that justice is another's good and the interest of the stronger, and that injustice is a man's own profit and interest, though injurious to the weaker. Now as you have admitted that justice is one of that highest class of goods which are desired indeed for their results, but in a far greater degree for their own sakes—like sight or hearing or knowledge or health, or any other real and natural and not merely conventional good—I would ask you in your praise of justice to regard one point only: I mean the essential good and evil which justice and injustice work in the possessors of them.

Let others praise justice and censure injustice, magnifying the rewards and honors of the one and abusing the other; that is a manner of arguing which, coming from them, I am ready to tolerate, but from you who have spent your whole life in the consideration of this question, unless I hear the contrary from your own lips, I expect something better. And therefore, I say, not only prove to us that justice is better than injustice, but show us how each of them effects the inner man, how it makes one man good and another man evil on the inside, whether seen or unseen by gods and men.

IV
Socrates

The meaning is, I believe, that in the human soul there is a better and also a worse principle; and when the better has the worse under control, then a man is said to be the master of himself; and this is a term of praise: but when, owing to bad education or associations, the better principle, which is also the smaller, is overwhelmed by the larger...

Then we may fairly assume that they are two, and that they differ from one another; the one with which man reasons, which we may call the rational principle of the soul, and the other, with which he hungers and thirsts and feels the fluttering of all other desires, may be termed the irrational or the appetitive, the ally of various pleasures and satisfactions?

Yes, he said, we may fairly assume them to be different.

Then let us finally determine that there are two

principles existing in the soul. But what of passion, or spirit? Is it a third, or akin to one of the preceding?

I should be inclined to say—akin to desire.

Well, I said, there is a story I remember to have heard which might best illustrate this. The story is, that Leontius, the son of Aglaion, coming up one day from the Piraeus, under the north wall on the outside, observed some dead bodies lying on the ground at the place of execution. He felt a desire to see them, and also a dread and abhorrence of them; for a time he struggled and covered his eyes, but at length the desire got the better of him; and forcing them open, he ran up to the dead bodies, saying, look, you wretches, and take your fill of the fair sight.

I have heard the story myself, he said.

The moral of the tale is, that anger at times goes to war with desire, as though they were two distinct things.

Yes; that is the meaning, he said.

And are there not many other cases in which we observe that when a man's desires violently prevail over his reason, he reviles himself, and is angry at the violence within him, and that in this struggle, which is like the struggle of the factions within a state, his spirit is on the side of his reason;—but for the passionate or spirited element to take part with the appetitive with reason not choosing to opposed, is a sort of thing which I believe you never have observed occurring in yourself, nor, as I should imagine, in any one else?

Certainly not.

Suppose that a man thinks he has done a wrong to another, the nobler he is the less able he is to feel indignant at any suffering, such as hunger, or cold, or any other pain which the injured person may inflict upon him—these he deems to be just, and, as I say, his anger refuses to be excited by them.

True, he said.

But when he thinks he is being made to suffer wrongly, he becomes angry, for he believes himself to be on the side of justice; and because he suffers hunger or cold or other pain he is all the more determined to persevere and conquer. His noble spirit will not be quelled until he either slays or is slain; or until he hears the voice of the shepherd, that is, reason, bidding his anger subside like a shepherd bids his dog bark no more.

Yes, he said. The illustration is perfect.

I perceive, I said, that you quite understand me; there is, however, a further point which I wish you to consider.

What point?

You remember that passion or spirit appeared at first sight to be a kind of desire, but now we should say quite the contrary; for in the conflict of the soul spirit is arrayed on the side of the rational principle.

Most assuredly.

But a further question arises: Is passion different from reason also, or only a kind of reason; in the latter case, instead of three principles in the soul, there will only be only two, the rational and the appetitive; or rather, as the state was composed of three classes, traders, auxiliaries, counsellors, so may there not be in the individual soul a third element which is the spirited, and when not corrupted by bad education is the natural ally of reason?

Yes, he said, there must be a third.

Yes, I replied, if the spirited, which has already been shown to be different from desire, turns out also to be different from reason.

But that is easily proved, he said, we may observe even in young children that they are full of spirit almost as soon as they are born, whereas some of them never seem to attain to the use of reason, and most of them late enough.

Excellent, I said, and you may see the spirited equally in brute animals, which is a further proof of the truth of what you are saying. And we may once more appeal to the words of Homer, which have been already quoted by us; 'He smote his breast, and thus rebuked his soul.' For in this verse Homer has clearly supposed the power of reason about the better and worse to be different from the unreasoning anger which is rebuked by it.

Very true, he said...

We must then recollect that the individual in whom the several qualities of his nature are balanced will be just, and will do his own work?

Yes, he said, we must remember that too.

And ought not the rational principle, which is wise, and has the care of the whole soul rule, and the passionate or spirited principle be its subject and ally?

Certainly.

And, as we were saying, the united influence of music and gymnastic will bring them into accord, nurturing and sustaining reason with noble words and lessons, and moderating and soothing and civilizing the wildness of the spirited by harmony and rhythm?

Quite true, he said.

And these two, thus nurtured and educated, and having learned truly to know their own functions, will rule over the appetitive, which in each of us is the largest part of the soul and by nature most insatiable for gain; over this they will keep guard, lest, waxing great and strong with the fullness of bodily pleasures, as they are termed, the appetitive soul, no longer confined to its own sphere, will attempt to enslave and rule over those who are not its subjects, and overturn the whole life of man?

Very true, he said.

Both together will they not be the best defenders of the whole soul and the whole body against attacks from without; the one counselling, and the other fighting under its leadership, and courageously executing its commands and counsels?

True.

And he is to be deemed courageous whose spirit retains in pleasure and in pain the commands of reason about what he ought or ought not to fear?

Right, he replied.

And him we call wise who has in him that little part which rules, and which proclaims these commands; that part too being supposed to have a knowledge of what is in the interest of each of the three parts and of the whole?

Assuredly.

And would you not say that he is temperate who has these same elements in friendly harmony, in whom the one ruling principle of reason, and the two subject ones of the spirited and the appetitive are equally agreed that reason ought to rule, and do not rebel?

Certainly, he said, that is the true account of temperance...

But in reality justice is such as we were describing, being concerned however, not with the outward man, but with the inward, which is the true self and concern of man: for the just man does not permit the several elements within him to interfere with one another, or any of them to do the work of the others,—he sets in order his own inner life, and he is his own master and his own law, and at peace with himself; and when he has bound together the three principles within him, that may be compared to the higher, lower, and middle notes of the scale, and the intermediate intervals—when he has bound all these together, and is no longer a man of many natures, but has become one entirely temperate and perfectly balanced nature, then he proceeds to act, if he has to act, whether in the matter of property, or in the treatment of the body, or in some affair of politics or private business; always thinking and calling that which preserves and co-operates with this harmonious condition, just and good action, and the knowledge that presides over it, wisdom, and that which at any time impairs this condition, he will call unjust action, and the opinion that presides over it ignorance.

You have said the exact truth, Socrates...

Then virtue is the health and beauty and well-being of the soul, and vice the disease and weakness and deformity of the soul?

True.

And do not good practices lead to virtue, and evil practices to vice?

Assuredly.

Still our old question of the comparative advantage of justice and injustice has not yet been answered: Which is the more profitable, to be just and act justly and practice virtue, whether seen or unseen by gods and men, or to be unjust and act unjustly, even if unpunished and unreformed?

In my judgment, Socrates, the question has now become ridiculous. We know that, when the bodily constitution is gone, life is no longer endurable, though pampered with all kinds of meats and drinks, and having all wealth and all power; and shall we be told that when the very balance of the vital principle is undermined and corrupted, life is still worth living to a man, if only he be allowed to do whatever he likes with the single exception that he is not to acquire justice and virtue, or to escape from injustice and vice; assuming them both to be such as we have described?

Yes, I said, the question is, as you say, ridiculous.

Still, as we are near the spot at which we may see the truth in the clearest manner with our own eyes, let us not faint by the way…

IX

Well, I said, and now having arrived at this stage of the argument, we may revert to the words which brought us here: Was not someone saying that injustice was a gain to the perfectly unjust man who was reputed to be just?

Yes, that was said.

Now then, having determined the power and quality of justice and injustice, let us have a little conversation with him.

What shall we say to him?

Let us make an image of the soul, that he may have his own words presented before his eyes.

Of what sort?

An ideal image of the soul, like the composite creations of ancient mythology, such as the Chimera or Scylla or Cerberus, and there are many others in which two or more different natures are said to grow into one.

There are said to have been such unions.

Then now model the form of a large, many-headed beast, having a ring of heads of all manner, some tame and some wild, which he is able to generate and make appear at will.

You suppose marvelous powers in the artist; but, as language is more pliable than wax or any similar substance, let there be such an image as you propose.

Suppose now that you make a second image as of a lion, and a third of a man, the second smaller than the first, and the third smaller than the second.

That, he said, is an easier task; and I have made them as you say.

Next fashion the outside of them into a single image, as of a man, so that he who is not able to look within, and sees only the outer image, may believe it to be a single human creature. I have done so, he said.

And now, to him who maintains that it is

profitable for a human being to be unjust, and unprofitable to be just, let us reply that, if he is right, it is profitable for this creature to feed the many-headed beast and strengthen the lion and the lion-like qualities, but to starve and weaken the man of reason, who is then liable to be dragged about at the mercy of either of the other two; and he is not to attempt to balance or harmonize them with one another—he ought rather to suffer them to fight and bite and devour one another.

Certainly, he said; that is what the approver of injustice says.

To him the supporter of justice makes answer that he should ever speak and act as to give the man within him in some way or other the most complete mastery over the entire human being.

He should watch over the many-headed beast like a good caretaker, fostering and cultivating the gentle qualities, and preventing the wild ones from growing; he should make the lion his ally, and in common care of them all should be balancing the several parts with one another and with himself.

Yes, he said, that is quite what he who maintain justice would say.

And so from every point of view, whether of pleasure, honor, or advantage, the approver of justice is right and speaks the truth, while the disapprover of justice is wrong and ignorant.

Yes Socrates, from every point of view.[ii]

NICOMACHEAN ETHICS
by Aristotle
I

Every art, every teachable science, and in like manner every action and moral choice, aims, it is thought, at some good. For this reason a common, and by no means bad, description of the final good is, "that which all things aim at."

Now there plainly is a difference in the ends proposed: for in some cases they are acts of working, and in others certain works or tangible results beyond and beside the acts of working: and where there are certain ends beyond and beside the actions, the works are in their nature better than the acts of working. Again, since actions and arts and sciences are many, the ends likewise come to be many. For example, the end of the healing art is health; the end of the ship-building art is a vessel; the end of the military art is victory; and the end of domestic management is wealth.

And whichever of such actions, arts, or sciences range under them (as under that of horsemanship the art of making bridles, and all that are connected with the manufacture of horse-tack in general), in all such cases the ends of the higher arts are always more choice-worthy than those under them, because it is with a view to the former that the latter are pursued.

Since then of all things that may be done there is

some one end which we desire for its own sake, and with a view to which we desire everything else; and since we do not choose in all instances with a further end in view (for this would go on to infinity, and so the desire would never be satisfied and fruitless), this plainly must be the final good—the best thing of all.

Surely then, even with reference to actual life and conduct, the knowledge of it must have great weight; and like archers, with a target to shot at, we shall be more likely to hit upon what is right: and if so, we ought to try to describe, in outline at least, what it is and of which of the sciences it is the end.

Now one would naturally suppose it to be the end of that which is most commanding and most inclusive: and to this description, plainly answers: for this determines which of the sciences should be in communities, and which kind of individuals should learn them, and what degree of proficiency is to be required. Again; we see also ranging under this the most highly esteemed sciences, such as the military arts, and that of domestic management, and rhetoric. Since this uses all of the other practical sciences, and moreover lays down rules as to what men are to do, and from what to abstain, the end of this must include the ends of the rest, and so must be the good of man. And grant that this is the same to the individual and to the community, yet surely that of the latter is plainly greater and more perfect to discover and preserve: for to do this even for a single individual is a matter for contentment; but to do it for a whole nation, and for communities in general, is more noble and godlike…

And now, resuming the statement with which we started, since all knowledge and moral choice grasps at a good of some kind, what good is that which we say it aims at? Or, in other words, what is the highest of all goods achievable by action?

So far as name goes, there is a pretty general agreement that it is happiness, as both the multitude and the refined few call it, and "living well" and "doing well" they conceive to be the same as "being happy;" but about the nature of this happiness, men dispute, and the multitude do not in their account of it agree with the wise. For some say it is one of those things which is palpable and apparent, like pleasure or wealth or honor; in fact, some think one thing, some another; and often the same man gives a different account of it; for when ill, he calls it health; when poor, wealth: and, conscious of their own ignorance, men admire those who talk grandly and above their comprehension. Some again hold it to be something by itself, other than and besides these many good things, which is the underlying cause of their being good.

Now to consider all opinions would perhaps be rather a fruitless task; so it shall suffice to consider those which are most generally professed, or are thought to have some reason in them...

Now of the final good men seem to form their notions from the different modes of life, as we might naturally expect: the vulgar masses conceive it to be pleasure, and hence they are content with the life of sensual enjoyment. For there are three types of life which stand out prominently in view: the life of pleasure, the life of politics, and the life of contemplation.

Now the vulgar masses are plainly quite slavish, choosing a life like that of brute animals: yet they obtain some consideration, because many of the great share the tastes of Sardanapalus. The refined and active again conceive it to be honor: for this may be said to be the end of the life of politics: yet this is plainly too superficial for the object of our search, because it is thought to rest with those who give honor rather than with those who receive it, for the final good we feel instinctively must be something that is intrinsic to us, and thus not easily taken away.

And besides, men seem to pursue honor, that they may believe themselves to be good: for instance, they seek to be honored by the wise, and by those among whom they are known, and for virtue: clearly then, in the opinion at least of these men, virtue is higher than honor. In truth, one would be much more inclined to think this to be the end of the life of politics; yet this itself is plainly not sufficiently final: for it is conceived possible, that a man possessed of virtue might sleep or be inactive all through his life, or, as a third case, suffer the greatest evils and misfortunes: and the man who should live thus no one would call happy, except for mere disputation's sake...

A third line of life is that of contemplation, of which we shall make our examination later.

As for the life of money-making, it is one of constraint, and wealth manifestly is not the good we are seeking, because it is for use, that is, for the sake of something else: and hence one would rather conceive the aforementioned ends to be the right ones, for men rest content with them for their own sakes. Yet, clearly, they are not the objects of our search either, though many words have been wasted on them. So much then for these...

And now let us return to the good of which we are searching. What can it be? For manifestly it is different in different actions and arts. For it is different in the healing arts and in the military arts, and similarly in the rest. What then is the final good in each? Is it not "that for the sake of which the other things are done?" and this in the healing arts is health, and in the military arts victory, and in that of house-building, a house, and in any other thing something else; in short, in every action and moral choice there is an end. So that if there is some one end of all of these things which are and may be done, this must be the good we are looking for.

Thus our discussion after some traversing about has come to the same point which we reached before. And this we must now try even more to clear up.

Now since the ends are plainly many, and of these we choose some with a view to others it is clear that all are not final: but the final good is manifestly something final; and so, if there is some one and only end that is final, this must be the object of our search: but if several, then it will be the most final of them.

Now that which we seek for itself we call more final than that which is sought with a view to something else. And that which is never an object of choice with a view to something else is thought greater than that which is only valued with a view to something else: and so by the term "absolutely final," we denote that which is an object of choice always in itself, and never with a view to something else.

And of this nature happiness is most thought to be, for this we choose always for its own sake, and never with a view to anything further: whereas honor, pleasure, intellect, in fact every excellence we choose for its own sakes we also choose with a view to happiness, conceiving that by using them as instruments we shall become happy: but no man chooses happiness with a view to them, nor in fact with a view to any other thing whatsoever.

The same result is seen to follow also from the notion of self-sufficiency, a quality thought to belong to the final good. Now by sufficient for self, we mean not for a single individual living a solitary life, but for his parents also and children and wife, and, in general, friends and countrymen; for man is by nature adapted to a social existence. But of these, of course, some limit must be fixed: for if one extends it to parents and descendants and friends' friends, there is no end to it. This point must be left for future investigation: for the present we define that to be self-sufficient which taken alone makes life choice-worthy, and to be in want of nothing; now of such kind we think happiness to be: and further, to be most choice-worthy of all things; not being compared with any other thing, for if we were to make such a comparison we would only find that happiness is always the greatest good.

So then happiness is manifestly something final and self-sufficient, being the end of all things which are and may be done.

But, it may be, to call happiness the final good is a mere truism, and what is wanted is some clearer account of its real nature. Now this object may be easily attained, when we have discovered what the work of man is; for as in the case of the flute-player, sculpture, or artisan of any kind, or, more generally, all who have any work or course of action, their final good and excellence is thought to reside in their work, so it would seem to be with man, if there is any work belonging to him.

Are we then to suppose, that while the carpenter and cobbler have certain works and courses of action, man as man alone has none, but is left by nature without a work? Or would not one rather hold, that as eye, hand, and foot, and generally each of his members, has some special work; so too the whole man, as distinct from all of these, has some work of his own?

What then can this be? Not merely the life of nourishment and growth, because that plainly is shared with plants and vegetables, and we want what is peculiar to man. We must separate off then the life of mere nourishment and growth, and next will come the life of sensation: but this again is commonly shared by horses, oxen, and every other animal. There remains then a rational life of an active nature: and of this nature there are two parts called rational, the one being obedient to reason, the other as having and exerting it. Again, as this life is also spoken of in two ways, we must focus on that which is in the way of actual working, because this is thought to be most properly entitled to the name. If then the work of man is a working of the soul in accordance with reason, or at least not independently of reason, and we say that the work of any given subject, and of that subject good of its kind, are the same in kind (as, for instance, of a harp-player and a good harp-player, and so on in every case, adding to the work eminence in the way of excellence; I mean, the work of a harp-player is to play the harp, and of a good harp-player to play it well); if, I say, this is so, and we assume that the work of man is to be life of a certain kind, that is to say a working of the soul, and actions with reason, and of a good man to do these things well and nobly, and in fact everything is finished off well in the way of the excellence which peculiarly belongs to it: if all this is so, then the good of man is "a working of the soul in the way of excellence," or, if excellence admits of degrees, in the way of the best and most perfect excellence.

And we must add, in a complete life; for as it is not one fine day that makes a spring, so it is not one day or a short time that makes a man blessed and happy...

We must now inquire concerning happiness, not only from our own conclusion and the data on which our reasoning proceeds, but also likewise from what is commonly said about it: because with the truth there is always a harmony, and with falsehood a disharmony.

Now there is a common division of goods into three classes; one being called external, the other two respectively those of the soul and body, and those belonging to the soul we call most properly and especially good. Well, in our definition we assume that the actions and workings of the soul constitute happiness, and these of course belong to the soul.

And so our account is a good one, at least according to this opinion, which is of ancient date, and accepted by those who profess philosophy.

Rightly too are certain actions and workings said to be ends, for the goods of the soul should be internal rather than external. Agreeing also with our definition is the common notion that the happy man lives well and does well, for it has been stated by us to be pretty much a kind of living well and doing well.

But further, the points required in happiness are found in combination in our account of it.

For some think it is virtue, others practical wisdom, others a kind of natural philosophy; others that it is these or some combination of these with pleasure, or at least not independent of it; while others take it to be external prosperity.

Of these opinions, some rest on the authority of the majority, some on antiquity, and others on that of a few men of note: and it is not likely that these classes should all be wrong , but be right on at least some if not most.

Now with those who assert it to be virtue (excellence), or some kind of virtue, our account agrees: for working in the way of excellence surely belongs to excellence.

And there is an important difference between conceiving of the final good as a possession or as an activity, in other words, as a mere state or as a working. For the state or habit may possibly exist in a subject without effecting any good, as, for instance, in him who is asleep, or in any other way inactive; but the working cannot be so, for it will of necessity act, and act well. And as at the Olympic Games it is not the finest and strongest men who are crowned, but they who enter the race, for out of these the champions are selected; so too in life, of the honorable and the good, it is only they who act that rightly win the prizes.

Their life too is in itself pleasant: for the feeling of pleasure is a mental sensation, and each feels pleasure at what he is said to be fond of: a horse, for instance, to him who is fond of horses, and a sight to him who is fond of sights: and so in like manner just acts to him who is fond of justice, and more generally the things in accordance with virtue to him who is fond of virtue. Now in the case of the vulgar masses the things which they individually esteem pleasant clash, because they are not so by nature, but to the lovers of nobleness those things are pleasant which are so by nature: and the actions in accordance with virtue are of this kind, so that they are pleasant both to the man who performs them and also by nature in themselves.

So then their life has no need of pleasure as a kind of addition, but involves pleasure in itself. For, besides what I have just mentioned, a man is not a good man at all who feels no pleasure in noble actions, just as no one would call that man just who does not feel pleasure in just acts, or liberal who does not feel pleasure in liberal acts, and similarly in the case of the other virtues which might be enumerated: and if this is so, then the actions in accordance with virtue must be in themselves pleasurable. Then again they are certainly good and noble, and each of these in the highest degree; if we are to take as right the judgment of the good man, for he judges as we have said.

Happiness is then most excellent, most noble, and most pleasant, and these attributes are not separated as in the well-known Delian inscription: "Most noble is that which is most just, but best is health; and naturally most pleasant is the obtaining one's desires." For all these co-exist in the best acts of working: and we say happiness is the one that is the best of them all.

Still it is quite plain that it does require the addition of external goods, as we have said: because without such things it is impossible, or at least in all events not easy, to do noble acts: for friends, money, and political influence are in a manner instruments whereby many things are done. Some things seem to depend upon divine blessing; like good birth, for instance, or fine offspring, or even personal beauty: for he is not at all capable of happiness who is cursed in these. As we have said already, the addition of prosperity of this kind does seem necessary to complete the idea of happiness; thus some rank good fortune, and others virtue, with happiness.

The question is thus raised, whether it is a thing that can be learned, or acquired by habit or discipline of some other kind, or whether it comes in the way of divine grace, or even in the way of chance...

Having determined these points, let us examine with respect to happiness, whether it belongs to the class of things praiseworthy or things precious.

Now it is plain that everything which is a subject of praise is praised for being of a certain kind and bearing a certain relation to something else: for instance, the just, and the valiant, and generally the good man, and virtue itself, we praise because of the actions and the results: and the strong man, and the quick runner, and so forth, we praise for being of a certain nature and bearing a certain relation to something good and excellent (and this is illustrated by attempts to praise the gods; for they are presented in a ludicrous aspect by being referred to by human standards, and this results from the fact, that all praise does, as we have said, imply reference to a standard). Now if it is to such objects that praise belongs, it is evident that what is applicable to the best objects is not praise, but something higher and better: which is a plain matter of fact, for not only do we call the gods blessed and happy, but of the men who most nearly resemble the gods we also pronounce them blessed. And in like manner in respect of goods; no man thinks of praising happiness as he does the principle of justice, but calls it blessed, as being something more godlike and more excellent…

Moreover, since happiness is a kind of working of the soul in the way of perfect excellence, we must inquire concerning virtue: for through doing so we shall probably have a clearer view concerning happiness…

II

Virtue then is of two kinds, intellectual and moral: now intellectual virtue comes originally, and is increased subsequently, by teaching (for the most part that is), and therefore needs experience and time; while moral virtue comes through habit.

From this fact it is plain that not one of the moral virtues comes to be in us merely by nature: because if such things existed by nature, none could be changed by habit: a stone, for instance, by nature gravitating downwards, could never by habit be brought to ascend, not even if one were to try and accustom it by throwing it up ten thousand times;

nor in fact could anything whose nature is in one way be brought by habit to be in another. The virtues then come to be in us neither by nature, nor in spite of nature, but we are furnished by nature with a capacity for receiving them and are perfected in them through habit.

Again, in whatever cases we get things by nature, we get the faculties first and perform the acts afterwards; an illustration of this is the case of our bodily senses, for it was not from having often seen or heard that we got these senses, but just the reverse: we had them and so exercised them, but did not have them because we had exercised them. But the virtues we get by first performing single acts of work, which, again, is the case of other things, as in the arts; for what we have to make we learn how to make by making: men come to be builders, for instance, by building; harp-players, by playing the harp: exactly so, by doing just acts we become just; by doing the actions of self-mastery we come to be perfected in self-mastery; and by doing brave actions brave...

Again, every virtue is either produced or destroyed from and by the very same circumstances: art too in like manner; I mean it is by playing the harp that both the good and the bad harp-players are formed: and similarly builders and all the rest; by building well men will become good builders; by building badly bad ones: in fact, if this had not been so, there would have been no need of instructors, but all men would have been at once good or bad in their arts without them.

So too then is it with the virtues: for by acting in the various relations in which we are thrown with our fellow men, we come to be, some just, some unjust: and by acting in dangerous positions and being habituated to feel fear or confidence, we come to be, some brave, others cowards.

Similarly is it also with respect to the occasions of lust and anger: for some men come to be perfected in self-mastery and mild, while others have no self-control; the one class by behaving in one way, the other by behaving in another. Or, in one word, habits are produced from like actions: and so what we have to do is to give a certain character to these particular actions, because the habits formed correspond to the differences of these.

So then, whether we are trained this way or that way straight from childhood, makes not a small but an important difference, or rather I would say it makes all the difference...

Since then the object of the present treatise is not mere speculation, as it is of some others (for we are inquiring not merely that we may know what virtue is but that we may become virtuous, or else our inquiry is useless), we must consider as to how we are to do the particular actions, because, as we have just said, the quality of the habits which shall be formed depends on this…

First then this must be noted, that it is the nature of such things to be spoiled by defect and excess; as we see in the case of health and strength, for excessive training impairs the strength as well as deficient training: meat and drink, in like manner, in too great or too small quantities, impair the health: while in due proportion they cause, increase, and preserve it.

Thus it is the same with the habits of perfected self-mastery and courage and the rest of the virtues: for the man who flies from and fears all things, and never stands up against anything, comes to be a coward; and he who fears nothing, but goes at everything, comes to be rash. In like manner too, he that tastes of every pleasure and abstains from none comes to lose all self-control; while he who avoids all comes as it were to lose his faculties of perception: that is to say, the habits of perfected self-mastery and courage are spoiled by the excess and defect, but by the mean states are preserved.

Furthermore, not only do the origination and growth of the habits come from and by the same circumstances, but also the acts of working after the habits are formed will be exercised in the same way: for so it is also with those things which are more apparent, strength for instance: for this comes by taking plenty of food and doing plenty of work, and the man who has attained strength is best able to do these: and so it is with the virtues, for not only do we by abstaining from pleasures come to be perfected in self-mastery, but when we have come to be so we can best abstain from pleasures: similarly too with courage: for it is by accustoming ourselves to despise objects of fear and stand up against them that we come to be brave...

So then it seems every one possessed of skill avoids excess and defect and seeks for and chooses the mean, not the absolute mean, but the mean in relation to himself.

Now if all skill accomplishes well its work by keeping an eye on the mean, and bringing the works to this point it is common enough to say such works as are in a good state, that "one cannot add to or take anything from them," under the notion of excess or defect. And good artisans, as we say, work with their eye on this, and excellence, like nature, is more exact and better than any art in the world, so it must have an ability to aim at the mean.

It is moral excellence, i.e. virtue, of course which I mean, because this is concerned with feelings and actions, and in these there can be excess and defect and the mean: it is possible, for instance, to feel the emotions of fear, confidence, lust, anger, compassion, and pleasure and pain generally, too much or too little, and in either case wrongly; but to feel them at the right time, in the right way, towards the right person, for the right reason, as we should do is the mean, or in other words the best state, and this is the property of virtue.

In like manner too with respect to actions, there may be excess and defect and the mean. Now virtue is concerned with feelings and actions, in which the excess is wrong and the defect is blamed but the mean is praised and goes right; and both these circumstances belong to virtue.

Virtue then is in a sense a mean state, since it certainly has an aptitude for aiming at the mean.

Again, one may go wrong in many ways, but right only in one; and so the former is easy, the latter difficult; it is easy to miss the mark and hard to hit it: and for this reason both the excess and the defect belong to vice, and the mean state to virtue; for, as the poet says, "Men may be bad in many ways, But good in one alone." Virtue then is a state exercised by a deliberate choice, being in relation to the mean, determined by reason, as the man of practical wisdom would determine it.

It is a middle state between too faulty ones, in the way of excess on one side and of defect on the other: because the faulty states on one side fall short of, and those on the other exceed, what is right, both in the case of the feelings and the actions; but virtue finds, and when found adopts, the mean.

And so, viewing it with respect to its essence and

definition, virtue is a mean state; but with reference to the final good and to excellence it is the highest state possible.

But it must not be supposed that every action or every feeling is capable of subsisting in this mean state, because some states immediately convey the notion of badness, like malevolence, shamelessness, and envy; and in the case of actions, adultery, theft, and murder; for all these and the like are in themselves bad.

In these then you never can go right, but must always be wrong: nor in such does the right or wrong depend on the selection of a proper person, time, or manner (take adultery for instance), but simply doing any one of these things is being wrong.

You might as well require that there should be determined a mean state, an excess and a defect in respect of acting unjustly, being cowardly, or giving up all control of the passions: for at this rate there will be of excess and defect a mean state; of excess, excess; and of defect, defect.

But just as of perfected self-mastery and courage there is no excess and defect, because the mean is in one point of view the highest possible state, so in neither of these faulty states can you have a mean state, excess, or defect, but however they are done they are wrong: you cannot, in short, have of excess, defect, or mean state in these; for there is no virtue in unjust acts.

It is not enough, however, to state this in general terms, we must also apply it to particular instances, because in treatises on moral conduct general statements have an air of vagueness, but those that go into detail are of greater reality: for the actions after all must be in detail, and the general statements, to be worth anything, must hold good here.

I. In respect of fears and confidence or boldness: The mean state is courage, the defect is to be a coward, and the excess is to be rash.

II. In respect of pleasures and pains (but not all, and perhaps fewer pains than pleasures): The mean state here is perfected self-mastery, the excess total absence of self-control. As for defect in respect of pleasure, we will call this insensibility.

III. In respect of giving and taking wealth: The mean state is liberality, the excess extravagance, and the defect stinginess: here each of the extremes involves really an excess and defect contrary to each other. I mean, the extravagant gives out too much and takes in too little, while the stingy man takes in too much and gives out too little...

Now that moral virtue is a mean state, and how it is so, and that it lies between two faulty states, one in the way of excess and another in the way of defect, and that is so because it has an tendency to aim at the mean both in feelings and in actions, all this has now been set forth fully and sufficiently.

And so it is hard to be good: for surely hard it is in each instance to find the mean, just as to find the mean point or centre of a circle is not what any man can do, but only one who knows how: just so to be angry, to give money, and handle expenses, is what any man can do, and easy: but to do these to the right person, in the right proportion, at the right time, with the right object, and in the right manner, this is not as before what any man can do, nor is it easy; and for this cause goodness is rare, praiseworthy, and noble.

IX

Now if happiness is a working in the way of excellence of course that excellence must be the highest, that is to say, the excellence of the best principle. Whether then this best principle is the intellect or some other thing that is thought naturally to rule and to lead and to conceive of noble and divine things, whether being in its own nature divine or the most divine of all our internal principles, the working of this in accordance with its own proper excellence must be perfect happiness.

That it is the contemplative life has been already stated: and this would seem to be consistent with what we said before and with truth: for, in the first place, this working is of the highest kind, since the intellect is the highest of our internal principles and the subjects with which it converses are the highest of all which fall within the range of our knowledge.

Next, it is also most continuous: for we are better able to contemplate than to do anything else whatsoever continuously.

Again, we think pleasure must be in some way an ingredient in happiness, and of all workings in accordance with excellence that in the way of philosophy is confessed to be the most pleasant: at least the pursuit of philosophy is thought to contain pleasures admirable for purity and permanence; and it is reasonable to suppose that its employment is more pleasant to those who have mastered it, than to those who are yet seeking it.

And the self-sufficiency which people speak of will attach chiefly to the contemplative life: of course the actual necessaries of life are alike needed by the philosopher, the just man, and all the other characters; but, supposing all sufficiently supplied with these, the just man needs people towards whom to practice his justice; and in like manner the man of perfected self-mastery, and the brave man, and so of the rest; whereas the philosopher can contemplate and speculate even when quite alone, and the more entirely he deserves the name the more able is he to do so: and although it may be that he can do better by having co-workers, he is still certainly most self-sufficient.

Also, happiness is thought to stand in perfect rest; for we toil that we may be at rest, and war that we may be at peace. Now all the practical virtues require either politics or war for their working, and the actions regarding these are thought to exclude rest; those of war entirely, because no one chooses war, nor prepares for war, for war's sake: he would indeed be thought a bloodthirsty villain who should make enemies of his friends to secure the existence of fighting and bloodshed. The working also of the statesman excludes the idea of rest, and, besides the actual work of government, seeks for power and dignities or at least happiness for the man himself and his fellow citizens: a happiness distinct from the national happiness which we evidently seek as being different and distinct.

If then of all of the actions in accordance with the various virtues those of politics and war are preeminent in honor and greatness, and these are restless, and aim at some further end and are not choice worthy for their own sakes, but the working of the intellect, being apt for contemplation, is thought to excel in earnestness, and to aim at no end beyond itself and to have pleasure of its own which helps to increase the working, and if the attributes of self-sufficiency, and capacity of rest, and tirelessness (as far as is compatible with human nature), and all other attributes of the highest happiness, plainly belong to this working, this must be perfect happiness, if attained in a complete duration of life (a condition added because none of the points of happiness can be incomplete).

Such a life will be higher than mere human nature, because a man will live like this not in so far as he is man but in so far as there is in him a divine principle. And in the proportion that this divine principle excels his human nature the working of its excellence shall excel that of any other excellence. Therefore, if pure intellect, as compared to human nature, is divine, so too, compared with man's ordinary life, will the life in accordance with it be.

Yet must we now give ear to those who bid us as humans to mind only human affairs, or as mortals only mortal things? Absolutely not! For as far as we can we must divinize ourselves and do all with a view to living in accordance with the highest principle in us, for small as it is in quantity, in the quality of its power and preciousness it far exceeds all others.

In fact this principle would seem to constitute each man's "self," since it is supreme and above all others in goodness it would be absurd then for a man not to choose his own life but that of some other.

And here will apply an observation made before, that whatever is proper to each is naturally best and most pleasant to him: such this is to man the life in accordance with pure intellect, and if so, this is also the happiest.[iii]

EPICURUS MORAL PHILOSOPHY
by Charles Bradlaugh

Epicurus was born in the early part of the year 344, B. C, the third year of the 109th Olympiad, at Gargettus, in the neighborhood of Athens. His father, Neocles, was of the Aegean tribe. Some allege that Epicurus was born in the island of Samos; but, according to others, he was taken there when very young by his parents, who formed a portion of a colony of Athenian citizens, sent to colonize Samos after its subjugation by Pericles. The father and mother of Epicurus were in very humble circumstances; his father was a schoolmaster, and his mother, Chærestrata, acted as a kind of priestess, curing diseases, exorcising ghosts, and exercising other fabulous powers.

At thirty-six years of age Epicurus returned to Athens. He purchased a pleasant garden, where he founded a school and taught his disciples until the time of his death. The better to prosecute his studies, Epicurus lived a life of celibacy. Temperate and continent himself, he taught his followers to be so likewise, both by example and precept. He died 273 B. C, in the seventy-third year of his age; and, at that time, his warmest opponents seem to have paid the highest compliments to his personal character.

The sum of his doctrine concerning philosophy, in general, is this:

Philosophy is the exercise of reason in the pursuit and attainment of a happy life; hence it follows, that those studies which are conducive neither to the acquisition or the enjoyment of happiness are to be dismissed as of no value. The end of all speculation ought to be, to enable men to judge with certainty what is to be chosen, and what is to be avoided, to preserve themselves free from pain, and to secure health of body, and tranquility of mind. True philosophy is so useful to every man, that the young should apply to it without delay, and the old should never be weary of the pursuit; for no man is either too young or too old to correct and improve his mind, and to study the art of happiness. Happy are they who possess by nature a free and vigorous intellect, and who are born in a country where they can prosecute their inquiries without restraint: for it is philosophy alone which raises a man above vain fears and base passions, and gives him the perfect command of himself. As nothing ought to be dearer to a philosopher than truth, he should, pursue it by the most direct means, devising no actions himself, nor suffering himself to be imposed upon by the fictions of others, neither poets, orators, nor logicians, making no other use of the rules of rhetoric or grammar, than to enable him to speak or write with accuracy and transparency, and always preferring a plain and simple to an ornamented style. While some doubt everything, and others profess to acknowledge everything, a wise man will embrace such tenets, and only such as are built upon experience, or upon certain and indisputable axioms.

The following is a summary of his Moral Philosophy:

The end of living, or the ultimate good, which is to be sought for its own sake, according to the universal opinion of mankind, is happiness; yet men, for the most part, fail in the pursuit of this end, either because they do not form a right idea of the nature of happiness, or because they do not make use of proper means to attain it. Since it is every man's interest to be happy through the whole of life, it is the wisdom of every one to employ philosophy in the search of happiness without delay; and there cannot be a greater folly, than to be always beginning to live.

The happiness which belongs to man, is that state in which he enjoys as many of the good things, and suffers as few of the evils common to human nature as possible; passing his days in a smooth course of permanent tranquility. A wise man, though deprived of sight or hearing, may experience happiness in the enjoyment of the good things which yet remain; and when suffering torture, or laboring under some painful disease, can mitigate the anguish by patience, and can enjoy, in his afflictions, the consciousness of his own constancy. But it is impossible that perfect happiness can be possessed without the pleasure which attends freedom from pain, and the enjoyment of the good things of life. Pleasure is in its nature good, as pain is in its nature evil; the one is, therefore, to be pursued, and the other to be avoided, for its own sake.

Pleasure, or pain, is not only good, or evil, in itself, but the measure of what is good or evil, in every object of desire or aversion; for the ultimate reason why we pursue one thing, and avoid another, is because we expect pleasure from the former, and pain from the latter. If we sometimes decline a present pleasure, it is not because we are averse to pleasure itself, but because we conceive, that the present pleasure will be necessarily followed by a greater pain. In like manner, if we sometimes voluntarily submit to a present pain, it is because we judge that it is necessarily connected with a greater pleasure. Although all pleasure is essentially good, and all pain essentially evil, it does not then necessarily follow, that in every single instance the one ought to be pursued, and the other to be avoided; but reason is to be employed in distinguishing and comparing the nature and degrees of each, that the result may be a wise choice of that which shall appear to be, upon the whole, good. That pleasure is the first good, appears from the inclination that every animal, from birth, pursues pleasure, and avoids pain; and this is confirmed by the universal experience of mankind, who are incited to action by no other principle than the desire of avoiding pain, or obtaining pleasure.

There are two kinds of pleasure: one consisting in a state of rest, in which both body and mind are undisturbed by any kind of pain; the other arising from an agreeable agitation of the senses, producing a correspondent emotion in the soul. It is upon the former of these that the enjoyment of life chiefly depends. Happiness may therefore be said to consist in bodily ease, and mental tranquility.

When pleasure is asserted to be the end of living, we are not then to understand this as the violent kinds of delight or joy which arises from the gratification of the senses and passions, but merely as that placid state of mind, which results from the absence of every cause of pain or uneasiness. Those pleasures, which arise from agitation, are not to be pursued as in themselves the end of living, but as a means of arriving at that stable tranquility, in which true happiness consists. It is the office of reason to confine the pursuit of pleasure within the limits of nature, in order for the attainment of that happy state, in which the body is free from every kind of pain, and the mind from all anxiety. This state must not, however, be conceived to be perfect in proportion to its inactivity, but in proportion to all of the functions of life being quietly and pleasantly performed. A happy life neither resembles a rapid torrent, nor a standing pool, but is like a gentle stream, that glides smoothly and silently along.

This happy state can only be obtained by a prudent care of the body, and a steady government of the mind. The diseases of the body are to be prevented by temperance, or cured by medicine, or rendered tolerable by patience. Against the diseases of the mind, philosophy provides sufficient antidotes. The instruments which it employs for this purpose are the virtues; the root of which, and of which all the rest proceed, is prudence. This virtue comprehends the whole art of living discreetly, justly, and honorably, and is, in fact, the same thing as wisdom. It instructs men to free their understandings from the clouds of prejudice; to exercise temperance and fortitude in the government of themselves: and to practice justice towards others. Although pleasure, or happiness, which is the end of living, is superior to virtue, which is only the means, it is in every one's interest to practice all of the virtues; for in a happy life, pleasure can never be separated from virtue.

A prudent man, in order to secure his tranquility, will consult his natural disposition in the choice of his plan for life. If, for example, he is persuaded that he should be happier in a state of marriage than in celibacy, he ought to marry; but if he be convinced that matrimony would be an impediment to his happiness, he ought to remain single. In like manner, such persons as are naturally active, enterprising, and ambitious, or such as by the condition of their birth are placed in the way of civil offices, should accommodate themselves to their nature and situation, by engaging in public affairs; while such as are, from natural temper, fond of leisure and retirement, or, from experience or observation, are convinced that a life of public service would be inconsistent with their happiness, are unquestionably at liberty, except where particular circumstances call them to the service of their country, to pass their lives in obscure repose.

Temperance is that discreet regulation of the desires and passions, by which we are enabled to enjoy pleasures without suffering any poor consequences. They who maintain such a constant self-command, as never to be enticed by the prospect of present indulgence, to do that which will be productive of evil, obtain the truest pleasure by declining pleasure. Since, of desires some are natural and necessary; others natural, but not necessary; and others neither natural nor necessary, but the offspring of false judgment; it must be the office of temperance to gratify the first class, as far as nature requires: to restrain the second within the bounds of moderation; and, as to the third, resolutely to oppose, and, if possible, entirely repress them.

Sobriety, as opposed to inebriety and gluttony, is of admirable use in teaching men that nature is satisfied with a little, and enabling them to content themselves with simple and frugal fare. Such a manner of living is conducive to the preservation of health: renders a man alert and active in all the offices of life; affords him an exquisite relish of the occasional varieties of a plentiful table, and prepares him to meet every reverse of fortune without the fear of want.

Continence is a branch of temperance, which prevents the diseases, infamy, remorse, and punishment, to which those are exposed, who indulge themselves in secret or illicit sex. Music and poetry, which are often employed as incentives to such sexual pleasures are to be cautiously and sparingly used.

Gentleness, as opposed to an irascible temper, greatly contributes to the tranquility and happiness of life, by preserving the mind from anxiety, and arming it against the assaults of calumny and malice. A wise man, who puts himself under the government of reason, will be able to receive an injury with calmness, and to treat the person who committed it with leniency; for he will rank injuries among the casual events of life, and will prudently reflect that he can no more stop the natural current of human passions, than he can curb the stormy winds. Obstinate servants in a family should be chastised, and disorderly members of a state punished without wrath.

Moderation, in the pursuit of honors or riches, is the only security against disappointment and vexation. A wise man will prefer the simplicity of rustic life to the magnificence of riches. Of future events he will consider uncertain, and will neither suffer himself to be elated with confident expectation, nor be depressed by doubt and despair: for both are equally destructive of tranquility. It will contribute to the enjoyment of life, to consider death as the perfect termination of a happy life, neither regretting the past, nor anxious for the future.

Fortitude, the virtue which enables us to endure pain, and to banish fear, is of great use in producing tranquility. Philosophy instructs us to pay homage to the gods, not through hope or fear, but from veneration of their superior nature. It moreover enables us to conquer the fear of death, by teaching us that it is no proper object of terror; since, while we are, death is not, and when death arrives, we are not: so that it neither concerns the living nor the dead. The only evils to be apprehended are bodily pain, and distress of mind. Of bodily pain it becomes a wise man to endure with patience and firmness; because, if it be slight, it may easily be borne; and if it be intense, it cannot last long. Mental distress commonly arises not from nature, but from opinion; a wise man will therefore arm himself against this kind of suffering, by reflecting that the gifts of fortune, the loss of which he may be inclined to deplore, were never his own, but depended upon circumstances which he could not command. If, therefore, they happen to leave him, he will endeavor, as soon as possible, to obliterate the remembrance of them, by occupying his mind in pleasant contemplation, and engaging in agreeable hobbies and advocations.

Justice respects man as living in society, and is the common bond without which no society can subsist. This virtue, like the rest, derives its value from its tendency to promote the happiness of life. Not only is it never injurious to the man who practices it, but nourishes in his mind calm reflections and pleasant hopes; whereas it is impossible that the mind in which injustice dwells, should not be full of anxiety. Since it is impossible that iniquitous actions should promote the enjoyment of life, as much as remorse of conscience, legal penalties, and public disgrace, must increase its troubles, everyone who follows the dictates of sound reason, will practice the virtues of justice, equity, and fidelity. In society, the necessity of the mutual exercise of justice, in order to the common enjoyment of the gifts of nature, is the ground of those laws by which it is prescribed. It is the interest of every individual in a state to conform to the laws of justice; for by injuring no one, and rendering to every man his due, he contributes his part towards the preservation of that society, upon the perpetuity of which his own safety depends. Nor ought any one to think that he is at liberty to violate the rights of his fellow citizens, provided he can do it securely; for he who has committed an unjust action can never be certain that it will not be discovered; and however successfully he may conceal it from others, this will avail him little, since he cannot conceal it from himself. In different communities, different laws may be instituted, according to the circumstances of the people who compose them. Whatever is thus prescribed is to be considered as a rule of justice, so long as the society shall judge the observance of it to be for the benefit of the whole. But whenever any rule of conduct is found upon experience not to be conducive to the public good, being no longer useful, it should no longer be prescribed.

Nearly allied to justice are the virtues of beneficence, compassion, gratitude, piety, and friendship. He who confers benefits upon others, procures to himself the satisfaction of seeing the stream of plenty spreading around him from the fountain of his beneficence; at the same time, he enjoys the pleasure of being esteemed by others. The exercise of gratitude, filial affection, and reverence for the gods, is necessary, in order to avoid the hatred and contempt of all men. Friendships are contracted for the sake of mutual benefit; but by degrees they ripen into such disinterested attachment, that they are continued without any prospect of advantage. Between friends there is a kind of league, that each will love the other as himself. A true friend will partake of the wants and sorrows of his friend, as if they were his own; if he be in want, he will relieve him; if he be in prison, he will visit him; if he be sick, he will come to him; situations may occur in which he might even die for him. It cannot then be doubted, that friendship is one of the most useful means of procuring a secure, tranquil, and happy life.

No man will, we think, find anything in the foregoing summary to justify the foul language used against Epicurus, and his moral philosophy.[iv]

ON THE HAPPY LIFE
by Seneca

To live happily, my brother Gallio, is the desire of all men, but their minds are blinded to a clear vision of just what it is that makes life happy; and so far from its being easy to attain the happy life, the more eagerly a man strives to reach it, the farther he recedes from it if he has made a mistake in the road; for when it leads in the opposite direction, his very speed will increase the distance that separates him.

First, therefore, we must seek what it is that we are aiming at; then we must look about for the road by which we can reach it most quickly, and on the journey itself, if only we are on the right path, we shall discover how much of the distance we overcome each day, and how much nearer we are to the goal toward which we are urged by a natural desire. But so long as we wander aimlessly, having no guide, and following only the noise and discordant cries of those who call us in different directions, life will be consumed in making mistakes — life that is brief even if we should strive day and night for sound wisdom. Let us, therefore, decide both upon the goal and upon the way, and not fail to find some experienced guide who has explored the region towards which we are advancing; for the conditions of this journey are different from those of most travel. On most journeys some well-recognized road and inquiries made of the inhabitants of the region prevent you from going astray; but on this one all the best beaten and the most frequented paths are the most deceptive.

Nothing, therefore, needs to be more emphasized than the warning that we should not, like sheep, follow the lead of the throng in front of us, travelling, thus, the way that all go and not the way that we ought to go. Yet nothing involves us in greater trouble than the fact that we adapt ourselves to common report in the belief that the best things are those that have met with the greatest approval — the fact that, having so many to follow, we live after the rule, not of reason, but of imitation. The result of this is that people are piled high, one above another, as they rush to destruction. And just as it happens that in a great crush of humanity, when the people push against each other, no one can fall down without drawing along another, and those that are in front cause destruction to those behind — this same thing, you may see happening everywhere in life.

No man can go wrong to his own hurt only, but he will be both the cause and the sponsor of another's wrongdoing. For it is dangerous to attach one's self to the crowd in front, and so long as each one of us is more willing to trust another than to judge for himself, we never show any judgment in the matter of living, but always a blind trust, and a mistake that has been passed on from hand to hand finally involves us and works our destruction. It is the example of other people that is our undoing; let us merely separate ourselves from the crowd, and we shall be made whole. But as it is, the populace, defending its own iniquity, pits itself against reason. And so we see the same thing happening that happens at the elections, where, when the fickle breeze of popular favor has shifted, the very same persons who chose the politicians wonder why those politicians were chosen. The same thing has one moment our favor, the next our disfavor; this is the outcome of every decision that follows the choice of the majority.

When the happy life is under debate, there will be no use for you to reply to me, as if it were a matter of votes: "This side seems to be in a majority." For that is just the reason it is the worse side. Human affairs are not so happily ordered that the majority prefer the better things; a proof of the worst choice is the crowd. Therefore let us find out what is best to do, not what is most commonly done — what will establish our claim to lasting happiness, not what finds favor with the rabble, who are the worst possible exponents of the truth.

But by the rabble I mean no less the servants of the court than the servants of the kitchen; for I do not regard the color of the garments that cloth the body. In rating a man I do not rely upon eyesight: I have a better and surer light, by which I may distinguish the false from the true. Let the soul discover the good of the soul. If the soul ever has leisure to draw breath and to retire within itself — ah! To what self-torture will it come, and how, if it confesses the truth to itself, it will say: "All that I have done up until now, I wish were undone; when I think of all that I have said, I envy the dumb; of all that I have prayed for, I rate my prayers as the curses of my enemies…

Why do I not rather seek some real good — one which I could feel, not one which I could display? These things that draw the eyes of men, before which they halt, which they show to one another in wonder, outwardly glitter, but are worthless within. Let us seek something that is a good in more than appearance — something that is solid, constant, and more beautiful in it's more hidden part; for this let us delve. And it is placed not far off; you will find it — you need only to know where to stretch out your hand. As it is, just as if we groped in darkness, we pass by things near at hand, stumbling over the very objects we desire.

Not to bore you with details, I shall pass over in silence the opinions of other philosophers, for it would be tedious to enumerate and refute them all. Do you listen to ours? But when I say ours, I do not bind myself to some particular one of the Stoic masters; I, too, have the right to form an opinion. Accordingly, I shall follow so-and-so, I shall request so-and-so to divide the question; perhaps, too, when called upon after all the rest, I shall impugn none of my predecessors' opinions, and shall say: "I simply have this much to add." Meantime, I follow the guidance of Nature — a doctrine upon which all Stoics are agreed. Not to stray from Nature and to mold ourselves according to her law and pattern — this is true wisdom.

The happy life, therefore, is a life that is in harmony with its own nature, and it can be attained in only one way. First of all, we must have a sound mind and one that is in constant possession of its sanity; second, it must be courageous and energetic, and, too, capable of the noblest fortitude, ready for every emergency, careful of the body and of all that concerns it, but without anxiety; lastly, it must be attentive to all the advantages that adorn life, but with over-much love for none — the user, but not the slave, of the gifts of Fortune. You understand, even if I do not say more, that, when once we have driven away all that excites or affrights us, there ensues unbroken tranquility and enduring freedom; for when pleasures and fears have been banished, then, in place of all that is trivial and fragile and harmful just because of the evil it works, there comes upon us first a boundless joy that is firm and unalterable, then peace and harmony of the soul and true greatness coupled with kindliness; for all ferocity is born from weakness.

It is possible also to define this good of ours in other terms — that is, the same idea may be expressed in different language. Just as an army remains the same, though at one time it deploys with a longer line, now is massed into a narrow space and either stands with hollowed center and wings curved forward, or extends a straightened front, and, no matter what its formation may be, will keep the selfsame spirit and the same resolve to stand in defense of the selfsame cause, — so the definition of the highest good may at one time be given in lengthy form, and at another be restrained and concise. So it will come to the same thing if I say: "The highest good is a mind that scorns the happenings of chance, and rejoices only in virtue," or say: "It is the power of the mind to be unconquerable, wise from experience, calm in action, showing the while much courtesy and consideration in relations with others." It may also be defined in the statement that the happy man is he who recognizes no good and evil other than a good and an evil mind — one who cherishes honor, is content with virtue, who is neither puffed up, nor crushed, by the happenings of chance, who knows of no greater good than that which he alone is able to bestow upon himself, for whom true pleasure will be the scorn of pleasures. It is possible, too, if one chooses to be discursive, to transfer the same idea to various other forms of expression without injuring or weakening its meaning. For what prevents us from saying that the happy life is to have a mind that is free, lofty, fearless and steadfast — a mind that is placed beyond the reach of fear, beyond the reach of desire, that counts virtue the only good, baseness the only evil, and all else but a worthless mass of things, which come and go without increasing or diminishing the highest good, and neither subtract any part from the happy life nor add any part to it?

A man thus grounded must, whether he wills or not, necessarily be attended by constant cheerfulness and a joy that is deep and issues from deep within, since he finds delight in his own resources, and desires no joys greater than his inner joys. Should not such joys as these be rightly matched against the paltry and trivial and fleeting sensations of the wretched body? The day a man becomes superior to pleasure, he will also be superior to pain; but you see in what wretched and baneful bondage he must linger whom pleasures and pains, those most capricious and tyrannical of masters, shall he be enslaved. Therefore we must make our escape to freedom. But the only means of procuring this is through indifference to fortune. Then will be born the one inestimable blessing, the peace and exaltation of a mind now safely anchored, and, when all error is banished, the great and stable joy that comes from the discovery of truth, along with kindliness and cheerfulness of mind; and the source of a man's pleasure in all of these will not be that they are good, but that they spring from a good that is his own.

Seeing that I am employing some freedom in treating my subject, I may say that the happy man is the one who is free from both fear and desire because of the gift of reason; since even rocks are free from fear and sorrow, and no less are the beasts of the field, yet for all that no one could say that these things are "blissful," when they have no comprehension of bliss. Put in the same class those people whose dullness of nature and ignorance of themselves have reduced them to the level of the beasts of the field and of inanimate things. There is no difference between the one and the other, since in one case they are things without reason, and in the other their reason is warped, and works their own hurt, being active in the wrong direction; for no man can be said to be happy if he has been thrust outside the pale of truth. Therefore the life that is happy has been founded on correct and trustworthy judgment, and is unalterable. Then, truly, is the mind unclouded and free from every ill, since it knows how to escape not only deep wounds, but even scratches, and, resolved to hold to the end whatever stand it has taken, it will defend its position even against the assaults of an angry fortune.

For so far as sensual pleasure is concerned, though it flows about us on every side, steals in through every opening, softens the mind with its blandishments, and employs one resource after another in order to seduce us in whole or in part, yet who of mortals, if he has left in him one trace of a human being, would choose to have his senses tickled night and day, and, forsaking the mind, devote his attention wholly to the body? "But the mind also," it will be said, "has its own pleasures." Let it have them, in sooth, and let it pose as a judge of luxury and pleasures; let it gorge itself with the things that are wont to delight the senses, then let it look back upon the past, and, recalling faded pleasures, let it intoxicate itself with former experiences and be eager now for those to come, and let it lay its plans, and, while the body lies helpless from present cramming, let it direct its thoughts to that to come — yet from all this, it seems to me, the mind will be more wretched than ever, since it is madness to choose evils instead of goods. But no man can be happy unless he is sane, and no man can be sane who searches for what will injure him in place of what is best.

The happy man, therefore, is one who has right judgment; the happy man is content with his present lot, no matter what it is, and is reconciled to his circumstances; the happy man is he who allows reason to fix the value of every condition of existence. Even those who declare that the highest good is in the belly see in what a dishonorable position they have placed it. And so they say that it is not possible to separate pleasure from virtue, and they aver that no one can live virtuously without also living pleasantly, nor pleasantly without also living virtuously. But I do not see how things so different can be cast in the same mold. What reason is there why pleasure cannot be separated from virtue? Do you mean, since all goods have their origin in virtue, even the things that you love and desire must spring from its roots? But if the two were inseparable, we should not see certain things pleasant, but not honorable, and certain things truly most honorable, but painful and capable of being accomplished only through suffering.

Then, too, we see that pleasure enters into even the basest life, but, on the other hand, virtue does not permit life to be evil, and there are people who are unhappy not without pleasure — nay, are so on account of pleasure itself — and this could not happen if pleasure were indissolubly joined to virtue; virtue often lacks pleasure, and never needs it. Why do you couple things that are unlike, nay, even opposites? Virtue is something lofty, exalted and regal, unconquerable, and unwearied; pleasure is something lowly, servile, weak, and perishable, whose haunt and abode are the brothel and the tavern. Virtue you will find in the temple, in the forum, in the senate-house — you will find her standing in front of the city walls, dusty and stained, and with calloused hands; pleasure you will more often find lurking out of sight, and in search of darkness, around the public baths and the sweating-rooms and the places that fear the police — soft, enervated, reeking with wine and perfume, and pallid, or else painted and made up with cosmetics like a corpse. The highest good is immortal, it knows no ending, it permits neither excess nor regret; for the right-thinking mind never alters, it neither is filled with self-loathing nor suffers any change in its life, that is ever the best. But pleasure is extinguished just when it is most enjoyed; it has but small space, and thus quickly fills it — it grows weary and is soon spent after its first assault. Nor is anything certain whose nature consists in movement. So it is not even possible that there should be any substance in that which comes and goes most swiftly and will perish in the very exercise of its power; for it struggles to reach a point at which it may cease, and it looks to the end while it is beginning.

What, further, is to be said of the fact that pleasure belongs alike to the good and the evil, and that the base delight no less in their disgrace than do the honorable in fair repute? And therefore the ancients have enjoined us to follow, not the most pleasant, but the best life, in order that pleasure should be, not the leader, but the companion of a right and proper desire. For we must use Nature as our guide; she it is that reason heeds, it is of her that it takes counsel. Therefore to live happily is the same thing as to live according to Nature. What this is, I shall proceed to make clear. If we shall guard the endowments of the body and the needs of Nature with care and fearlessness, in the thought that they have been given but for a day and are fleeting, if we shall not be their slaves, nor allow these alien things to become our masters, if we shall count that the gratifications of the body, unessential as they are, have a place like to that of the auxiliaries and light-armed troops in camp — if we let them serve, not command — thus and thus only will these things be profitable to the mind. Let a man not be corrupted by external things, let him be unconquerable and admire only himself, courageous in spirit and ready for any fate, let him be the molder of his own life; let not his confidence be without knowledge, nor his knowledge without firmness; let his decisions once made abide, and let not his decrees be altered by any erasure. It will be understood, even without my adding anything, that such a man will be poised and well ordered, and will show majesty mingled with courtesy in all his actions. Let reason search into external things at the instigation of the senses, and, while it derives from them its first knowledge — for it has no other base from which it may operate, or begin its assault upon truth — yet let it fall back upon itself.

For God also, the all-embracing world and the ruler of the universe, reaches forth into outward things, yet, withdrawing from all sides, returns into himself. And our mind should do the same; when, having followed the senses that serve it, it has through them reached to things without, let it be the master both of them and of itself. In this way will be born an energy that is united, a power that is at harmony with itself, and that dependable reason which is not divided against itself, nor uncertain either in its opinions, or its perceptions, or in its convictions; and this reason, when it has regulated itself, and established harmony between all its parts, and, so to speak, is in tune, has attained the highest good. For no crookedness, no slipperiness is left to it, nothing that will cause it to stumble or fall. It will do everything under its own authority and nothing unexpected will befall it, but whatever it does will turn out a good, and that, too, easily and readily and without subterfuge on the part of the doer; for reluctance and hesitation are an indication of conflict and instability. Wherefore you may boldly declare that the highest good is harmony of the soul; for where concord and unity are, there must the virtues be. Discord accompanies the vices.

"But even you," it is retorted, "cultivate virtue for no other reason than because you hope for some pleasure from it." But, in the first place, even though virtue is sure to bestow pleasure, it is not for this reason that virtue is sought; for it is not this, but something more than this that she bestows, nor does she labor for this, but her labor, while directed toward something else, achieves this also. As in a plowed field, which has been broken up for corn, some flowers will spring up here and there, yet it was not for these poor little plants, although they may please the eye, that so much toil was expended — the sower had a different purpose, these were superadded — just so pleasure is neither the cause nor the reward of virtue, but its by-product, and we do not accept virtue because she delights us, but if we accept her, she also delights us. The highest good lies in the very choice of it, and the very attitude of a mind made perfect, and when the mind has completed its course and fortified itself within its own bounds, the highest good has now been perfected, and nothing further is desired; for there can no more be anything outside of the whole than there can be some point beyond the end. Therefore you blunder when you ask what it is that makes me seek virtue; you are looking for something beyond the supreme. Do you ask what it is that I seek in virtue? Only herself. For she offers nothing better — she herself is her own reward. Or does this seem to you too small a thing? When I say to you, "The highest good is the inflexibility of an unyielding mind, its foresight, its sublimity, its soundness, its freedom, its harmony, its beauty, do you require of me something still greater to which these blessings may be ascribed?

Let them cease, therefore, to join irreconcilable things and to link pleasure with virtue — a vicious procedure which flatters the worst class of men. The man who has plunged into pleasures, in the midst of his constant belching and drunkenness, because he knows that he is living with pleasure, believes that he is living with virtue as well; for he hears first that pleasure cannot be separated from virtue, then dubs his vices wisdom, and parades what ought to be concealed. And so it is not Epicurus who has driven them to debauchery, but they, having surrendered themselves to vice, hide their debauchery in the lap of philosophy and flock to the place where they may hear the praise of pleasure, and they do not consider how sober and abstemious the "pleasure" of Epicurus really is — for so, in all truth, I think it — but they fly to a mere name seeking some justification and screen for their lusts. And thus they lose the sole good that remained to them in their wickedness — shame for wrong-doing. For they now praise the things that used to make them blush, and they glory in vice; and therefore they cannot even recover their youth, when once an honorable name has given warrant to their shameful laxity. The reason why your praise of pleasure is harmful is that what is honorable in your teaching lies hidden within, while what corrupts is plainly visible.

Personally I hold the opinion — I shall express it though the members of our school may protest — that the teachings of Epicurus are upright and holy and, if you consider them closely, austere; for his famous doctrine of pleasure is reduced to small and narrow proportions, and the rule that we Stoics lay down for virtue, this same rule he lays down for pleasure — he bids that it obey Nature. But it takes a very little luxury to satisfy Nature! What then is the case? Whoever applies the term "happiness" to slothful idleness and the alternate indulgence in gluttony and lust, looks for a good sponsor for his own evil course, and when, led on by an attractive name, he has found this one, the pleasure he pursues is not the form that he is taught, but the form that he has brought, and when he begins to think that his vices accord with the teacher's maxims, he indulges in them no longer timidly, but riots in them, not now secretly, but from this time on in broad daylight. And so I shall not say, as do most of our sect, that the school of Epicurus is an academy of vice, but this is what I say — it has a bad name, is of ill repute, and yet undeservedly. How can anyone know this who has not been admitted to the inner shrine? Its mere outside gives ground for scandal and incites to evil hopes. The case is like that of a strong man dressed up in a woman's garb; you maintain your chastity, your virility is unimpaired, your body is free from base submission — but in your hand is a tambourine! Therefore, you should choose some honorable superscription and a motto that in itself appeals to the mind; the one that stands has attracted only the vices.

Whosoever has gone over to the side of virtue, has given proof of a noble nature; he who follows pleasure is seen to be weak, broken, effeminate, and on the sure path to baseness unless someone shall establish for him some distinction between pleasures, so that he may know which of them lies within the bounds of natural desire, and which sweep onward and are unbounded and are the more insatiable the more they are satisfied. Come then! Let virtue lead the way, and every step will be safe. Then, too, it is the excess of pleasure that harms; but in the case of virtue there need be no fear of any excess, for in virtue itself resides moderation. That cannot be a good that suffers from its own magnitude. Besides, to creatures endowed with a rational nature what better guide can be offered than reason? Even if that combination pleases you, if you are pleased to proceed toward the happy life in such company, let virtue lead the way, let pleasure attend her — let it hover about the body like its shadow. To hand over virtue, the loftiest of mistresses, to be the handmaid of pleasure is the part of a man who has nothing great in his soul.

Therefore let the highest good mount to a place from which no force can drag it down, where neither pain nor hope nor fear finds access, nor does any other thing that can lower the authority of the highest good; but virtue alone is able to mount to that height. We must follow her footsteps to find that ascent easy; bravely will she stand, and she will endure whatever happens, not only patiently, but even gladly; she will know that every hardship that time brings comes by a law of Nature, and like a good soldier she will submit to wounds, she will count her scars, and, pierced by darts, as she dies she will love him for whose sake she falls — her commander; she will keep in mind that old injunction, "Follow God!" But whoever complains and weeps and moans, is compelled by force to obey commands, and, even though he is unwilling he is rushed none the less to the bidden tasks. But what madness to prefer to be dragged rather than to follow! As much so, in all faith, as it is great folly and ignorance of one's lot to grieve because of some lack or some rather bitter happening, and in like manner to be surprised or indignant at those ills that befall the good no less than the bad — I mean sickness and death and infirmities and all the other unexpected ills that invade human life. All that the very constitution of the universe obliges us to suffer, must be borne with high courage. This is the sacred obligation by which we are bound — to submit to the human lot, and not to be disquieted by those things which we have no power to avoid. We have been born under a monarchy; to obey God is freedom. Therefore true happiness is founded upon virtue. And what is the counsel this virtue will give to you? That you should not consider anything either a good or an evil that will not be the result of either virtue or vice; then, that you should stand unmoved both in the face of evil and by the enjoyment of good, to the end that — as far as is allowed — you may body forth God. And what does virtue promise you for this enterprise? Mighty privileges and equal to the divine. You shall be bound by no constraint, nothing shall you lack, you shall be free, safe, unhurt; nothing shall you essay in vain, from nothing be debarred; all things shall happen according to your desire, nothing adverse shall befall you, nothing contrary to your expectations and wish. "What! Does virtue alone suffice for living happily?" Perfect and divine as it is, why should it not suffice — nay, suffice to overflowing? For if a man has been placed beyond the reach of any desire, what can he possibly lack?[v]

THE HAPPY LIFE
by Augustine

The Happy Life (De beata vita) holds a unique place among the works of Augustine. Of all his writings handed down to posterity, it was the first one the great African completed. The year 386 was most important for Augustine's intellectual and spiritual development. Only a few months had passed since he had converted to Christianity, and now he was spending a vacation at Cassiciacum, a rural retreat near Milan, generously offered to him by his friend Verecundus, a grammarian of Milan and his colleague. Augustine had come to Cassiciacum seeking rest and peace.

He grasped the first opportunity to discuss with his friends the most innate desire and final goal of all human activity—happiness. The theme of the discussion in De beata vita is man's desire to be happy. This is an issue of fundamental importance in any man's life. Though men do not think of happiness in all their actions, yet everything they do is related to happiness. Augustine's philosophy differs from other philosophical systems in this respect: that it is not a neutral speculation and cold investigation of natural events or hypothetical problems, but tends to the welfare of the living man. Thus, the truth he is seeking is identical with the supreme good, the possession of which alone can completely satisfy all human searching and desire. To find this truth and to know what to do, to become always better and to reach finally the supreme good, man must know himself.

In De beata vita, then, Augustine has laid the foundation for, and indicated the outline of, his great theistic-democratic program, in which man, through individual ethical development in and for the welfare of the community, grows and gains a temporal and afterwards a perfect, eternal, happy life. For this reason, eminent scholars have acknowledged the importance of this early work of Augustine for the understanding of his personal development and his whole philosophy. It is in this little work that Augustine first seeks to establish the absolute certitude of one's own consciousness as the essential basis of knowledge, an original idea that became one of the greatest of Augustine's accomplishments.

The De beata vita is one of Augustine's works in which the title denotes a philosophical concept. The book evolves by dialectic argumentation and occasional application of metaphysical concepts, a definition of this concept. The procedure, as well as Augustine's general high regard for definition, division, and distinction and the frequent use of syllogism show the formal aspect of his mind and writings. The structure of the De beata vita is derived from Cicero. The latter's dialogue Hortensius (now lost) seems surely to have been a determining factor for the book's content and form. Augustine has added a novelty to the usual form of dialogue in introducing both a woman, his mother, and a child, his son, as taking active part in the discussion. He thus shows his conviction that philosophy is not the prerogative of a chosen few, but a common good of all persons irrespective of age, sex, ethnicity, or occupation.

Chapter 1

On the Ides of November fell my birthday. After a breakfast light enough not to impede our powers of thinking, I asked all those of us who, not only that day but every day, were living together to have a congenial session in the bathing quarters, a quiet place fitting for the season. Assembled there—for without hesitation I present them to your kindness, though only by name—were first, our mother, to whose merit, in my opinion, I owe everything that I live; my brother Navigius; Trygetius and Licentius, fellow citizens and my pupils; Lastidianus and Rusticus, relatives of mine, whom I did not wish to be absent, though they are not trained even in grammar, since I believed their common sense was needed for the difficult matter I was undertaking. Also my son, Adeodatus, the youngest of all, was with us, who promises great success, unless my love deceives me. While all these were paying attention, I started in the following manner.

Chapter 2

'We wish to be happy, do we not?'

No sooner had I said this, than they agreed, with one voice. I asked: 'In your opinion, is a person happy who does not possess what he wants?'

They said: 'By no means.'

'What? Everyone who possesses what he wants is happy?'

At this point our mother said: 'If he wishes and possesses good things, he is happy; if he desires evil things—no matter if he possesses them—he is wretched.'

I smiled at her and said cheerfully: 'Mother, you have really gained the mastery of the very stronghold of philosophy. For, undoubtedly you were wanting the words to express yourself like Tullius, who also has dealt with this matter. In his Hortensius, a book written in the praise and defense of philosophy he said:'

> Behold, not the philosophers, but only people who like to argue, state that all are happy who live according to their own will. This, of course, is not true, for, to wish what is not fitting is the worst of wretchedness. But it is not so deplorable to fail of attaining what we desire as it is to wish to attain what is not proper. For, greater evil is brought about through one's wicked will than happiness through fortune.

At these words our mother exclaimed in such a way that we, entirely forgetting her sex, thought we had some great man in our midst, while in the meantime I became fully aware where and from what divine source this flowed.

Then Licentius spoke up: 'You must tell us what a person has to wish in order to be happy, and what kind of things he must desire.'

'Invite me,' I said, 'to your birthday party, and I will accept gladly what you serve. In this manner, please, be my guest today and do not ask for something that is perhaps not prepared.'

When he felt sorry because of his request, though it was modest and not out of place, I asked: 'Do we all now agree that nobody can be happy without possessing what he desires, and that not everyone who has what he wants is happy?'

They all expressed their approval.

'But what about this?' I asked. 'Do you grant that everyone who is not happy is wretched?'

They had no doubt about this.

'Everyone, then,' I continued, 'who does not possess what he wants is miserable.'

All assented.

'But what preparations should a man make to gain happiness?' I asked. 'For this, perhaps, is also a question to serve up at our banquet, so that the eagerness of Licentius may not be disregarded. In my opinion, what a man possesses ought to be obtained by him when he wants it.'

'That is evident,' they said.

'It must be something,' I remarked, 'that ever remains, and is neither dependent upon fate nor subject to any mishap. For, whatever is mortal and transitory we cannot possess whenever we wish it, and as long as we wish to have it.'

All agreed.

But Tygetius said: 'Many favorites of fortune possess abundantly and plentifully those things which, though frail and subject to mishaps, are pleasant for the earthly life. And they lack nothing they desire.'

To him I replied: 'In your opinion, is a person happy who has fear?'

'It does not seem so,' he answered.

'If, then, someone is likely to lose what he loves, can he be without fear?'

'No,' he said.

'All those fortuitous things can be lost. No one, then, who possesses and loves them can ever be happy.'

He did not refute this.

At this point, however, our mother said: 'Even if somebody were certain that he would not lose all those things, he still could not be satisfied with such possessions. Hence, he is miserable because he is ever needy.'

'But, in your opinion would not someone be happy,' I asked, 'who has all these things in abundance and superfluity, if he is moderate in his desires, and enjoys them with contentment properly and presently?'

'In this case,' she replied, 'he is not happy through the possession of these things, but through the moderation of his mind.'

'Very well expressed,' I said. 'No better answer

to my question could be expected, and no other one from you. Therefore, we do not have the slightest doubt that anyone setting out to be happy must obtain for himself that which always endures and cannot be snatched away through any severe misfortune.'

Trygetius said: 'We have already agreed to this.'

'Is God, in your opinion, eternal and ever remaining?' I asked.

'This, of course, is so certain,' replied Licentius, 'that the question is unnecessary.' All the others agreed with pious devotion.

'Therefore,' I concluded, 'whoever possesses God is happy.'

As they readily and joyfully agreed to this, I continued: 'It seems to me, therefore, that we have only to inquire what man really possesses God, for he, certainly, will be happy. It is your opinion about this that I now ask.'

Here Licentius remarked: 'He who lives an upright life possesses God.'

Trygetius continued: 'He who does what God wills to be done possesses God.'

Lastidianus also agreed to this opinion.

The boy, the youngest of all, said, however: 'Whoever has a spirit free from uncleanness has God.'

Our mother approved all the answers, especially the last one.

Navigius remained silent. When I asked him what he thought, he replied that he was rather pleased with the last answer.

In order that Rusticus should not appear to be neglected in such an important matter, I asked him for his opinion, for it seemed to me that he kept silence not as much out of deliberation as through bashfulness. He agreed with Trygetius.

Then I said: 'Now I know the opinions of all on this most important matter. Beyond this question we have no need to inquire nor can anything be found, if only we continue our investigation, as we began, with the greatest serenity and sincerity. However, this investigation would be tedious today; for the mind also in its feasts may go to excess if it indulges too greedily in the meal—in this way it digests poorly, and the consequent discomfort is no less harmful to the health of the mind than the hunger itself. Therefore, if you do not object, we will rather take up this question tomorrow, when we are hungry again.'

<u>Chapter 3</u>

When we had convened again in the same room on the following day after breakfast, though a little later than the day before, I began:

'Who, in your opinion, possesses God?'

'If I remember correctly, three opinions were expressed on this point. The first preferred to think that one possesses God who does his will. Others, however, thought that a person who lived an upright life possesses God. Still others saw God in those souls that are free of unclean spirits.'

'But perhaps all of you have expressed the same opinion, only in different words. For, if we consider the first two statements—everyone who lives uprightly does what God wills, and everyone who does what God wills lives uprightly—we see that living an upright life is the same as doing what pleases God; unless this seems to you otherwise.'

They agreed.

'Now I intend to question you, rather briefly, about this point: whether God desires that man seek Him.'

They said: 'Yes.'

I also asked: 'Can we say that one who seeks God leads a bad life?'

'By no means,' was their reply.

'Answer me yet a third question: Is an impure spirit able to seek God?'

They said: 'No.' Navigius, still a little in doubt, at first, finally agreed with the others.

'If, then,' I said, 'one who seeks God obeys the will of God, he both lives righteously and is without an impure spirit. On the other hand, one who seeks God has not yet found God. Nothing, then, immediately compels our belief that whoever lives an upright life, or does what God wills, or has not an impure spirit, has God.'

While the others laughed at the fact that they were misled through their own admissions, our mother, stunned for a while, requested that through an explanation I should loosen and untangle for her the logical knot I had been compelled to present.

After this had been done, she said: 'But nobody can attain God without first seeking Him.'

'Very well,' I replied. 'But one who is still seeking has not yet attained God, although he lives an upright life. Therefore, not everyone who lives a good life possesses God.'

She then said: 'I believe that everyone possesses God, but, if one lives righteously, he has God favorable to him, and, if wrongly, hostile.'

'Incorrectly, then,' I said, 'we conceded yesterday that the one is happy who possesses God, since every man possesses God and not every man is happy.'

'Therefore, add the word 'favorable,' she said.

'Are we at least certain about the conclusion, that he is happy who has God favorable to him?' I asked.

'I should like to agree,' said Navigius, 'but I am afraid about the man who is still searching for God.'

'For it is impossible for me to say that God is unfavorable to the man who seeks him; and, if it is improper to say this, He will be favorable. But, whoever has God favorable to him is happy. The man who seeks is, therefore, happy, although everyone who seeks does not possess what he wants.'

'Thus, also, that man is happy who does not possess what he wants, a conclusion that appeared to be absurd to us all yesterday; whence we thought that we had dispersed this obscure teaching.'

At this point, when even our mother had smiled, Trygetius said; 'I do not at once concede that God is unfavorable to the one to whom He is not favorable. But I believe there is a middle state.'

I then asked him; 'Do you believe that such a man, to whom God is neither favorable nor hostile, still possesses God in some way?'

Since he was a little reluctant, our mother said; 'To possess God, and not to be without God, are two quite different things.'

'Which, then,' I asked, 'is better; to possess God, or not to be without God?'

'As far as I can see,' she replied, 'my opinion is this; He who lives righteously possesses God, that is, has Him propitious to him; he who lives a bad life also possesses God, but as hostile to him. But, whoever is still seeking God, and has not yet found Him, has Him neither as propitious nor as hostile, yet is not without God.'

'Is this also your opinion?' I asked the others.

They said; 'Yes.'

'Kindly tell me,' I urged; 'In your opinion, is not God more propitious to the one whom He favors?'

They acknowledged that it was so.

'Is God not favorable toward the man who is seeking Him?' I asked again.

'Yes,' they replied.

'Consequently, whoever seeks God has God propitious to him. But, everybody who has God propitious to him is happy. On the strength of this, also, one is happy who seeks God. But, whoever is seeking does not yet possess what he wishes to possess. Consequently, he is happy who does not possess what he wants to possess.'

Our mother remarked; 'According to my view, by no means is one happy who does not possess what he wishes.'

'Then,' I said, 'not everybody is happy who has God propitious to him.'

'If reasoning demands this conclusion,' she replied, 'I cannot deny it.'

Then I said; 'We, therefore, have to make the following distinction; everyone is happy who has already found God and has God propitious to him; on the other hand, everyone who is seeking God has God propitious to him, but is not yet happy. Of course, everybody who, through vices and sins, goes astray from God is not only unhappy, but is not even living with God's favor.'

When it was approved by all, I continued. 'Very well; I am afraid only that you will be vexed through a conclusion already agreed upon, namely, that he is miserable who is not happy; for, thence it logically follows that that man is miserable who has God propitious to him, since—as we have said—he still seeks God and therefore is not yet happy. Or, indeed, should we, like Tullius, call the owners of large estates rich, but the possessors of all virtues poor? But consider whether, as it is true that every needy person is miserable, it is also true that every miserable one is needy. In this case, then, it will be correct to say that misery is but poverty, a statement which, after it is made, I now approve as you have heard.'

'However, the investigation of this would take too long for today. Thus, that you may not become dismayed, I ask you to meet again tomorrow at the same table.'

As soon as all had expressed their eagerness to comply with my request, we rose.

Chapter 4

On the third day of our discussion, the morning mist, which was keeping us in the bathing quarters, dispersed, and the weather gave us a very sunny afternoon. So we decided to go down to the little meadow nearby. After we were all seated in what seemed a comfortable spot, the remainder of our colloquy was taken up as follows.

I began; 'Almost everything which, in questioning you, I wanted you to concede, I have received and retained. Therefore I believe—since we are finally able to distinguish our session through a certain interval of days—there will be no need for you today to give me any answer or, at least, not many answers. However, our mother has stated that wretchedness is nothing but poverty, and we are all agreed also that all are wretched who are needy. But, whether also all who are wretched are in need is a question which we could not explain yesterday.

'If reason has demonstrated that this is so, then the question "Who is happy?" is perfectly solved; it will be the one who is not in need. For, everyone who is not miserable is happy. Therefore, happy is the man who is without need, if we are to say the need (*egesta*) is identified with misery (*miseria*).'

'Cannot the conclusion that everyone is happy who is not in need,' asked Trygetius, 'be drawn from the evident fact that every needy man is miserable? I remember that we agreed upon no middle state between the miserable and the happy.'

'In your opinion, does a middle state exist between a dead and a living man?' I asked. 'Is not every man either alive or dead?'

'I grant you that here also there is no middle state,' he replied, 'But to what avail is this?'

'Because,' I continued, 'I believe that you will also concede that a person is dead who has been buried for a year.'

He did not deny it.

'But, does it follow from this that also one is still living who has not been buried for a year?'

'This does not follow,' he said.

'Therefore, I continued, 'it does not follow, from the supposition that everyone is miserable who is in want, that everyone is happy who is not in want, although a middle state cannot any more be found between the miserable man and the happy than between a living man and a dead man.'

Because some of them grasped this rather slowly, I tried, as well as I could, to enlighten them by the use of words more suited to their understanding, and I said; 'No one has any doubt that everybody is miserable who is in want, and we are not discouraged by certain things necessary for the body, even of the wise. A soul in which the happy life resides is not in want of these things. For, the soul itself is perfect, and whatever is perfect is not in want of anything. However, it will take what it seems that the body needs, if such is available; if it is not available, its lack will not crush it.'

'Every wise man is strong, and the strong man entertains no fear. The wise man, therefore, is not afraid either of bodily death or of those pains for whose banishment, prevention, or delay he would need all those things of which he is capable of being in want.'

'Nevertheless, he will always make wise use of

them, when they are not wanting. For there is much truth in the statement, "To allow admittance to something you can avoid, is foolish."

'He will, therefore, shun death and pain, so far as it is possible and becoming to do so. Otherwise, that is, not taking any precaution at all, he may be miserable, not because these things happened to him, but because he took no care to avoid them when he could have done so—and this is certainly a sign of folly. Consequently, in not avoiding them, it is not through enduring them that he would be miserable, but through folly.'

'But if, in spite of most earnest and worthy efforts he cannot prevent those happenings, they will not make him miserable. And the following saying of the comedy is equally true: "Since not all you wish can be done, wish only what can be done."

'How will anyone be wretched to whom nothing happens contrary to his wish? For he cannot wish anything which he believes he cannot attain. He has thus set his will only on very definite things; that is, in whatever he undertakes, he acts either in conformity with virtuous duty or the divine law of wisdom, and these things can by no means be taken away from him.'

'But, now consider whether every wretched man is also in want. To admit this is rather difficult in view of the fact that many people live in the midst of fortune's abundant gifts, people for whom everything is pleasant and easy; whatever their passion desires is furnished immediately at their nod. Such a life, of course, is not easy to attain.

'But, let us think of such a man as resembles Tullius' description of Orata. Who could affirm offhand that Orata had been afflicted with want, since he was a man of great riches, luxuries, and delights, not lacking anything in regard to pleasure, influence, dignity, and having a healthy constitution? Immensely rich in estates, and exceptionally blessed with most charming friends, he had in abundance whatever his heart desired, and all these goods in the interest of his physical wellbeing. In a word, all his undertakings and his every wish were crowned with success.'

'Perhaps one of you may say that this man desired to have more than he actually had. But this is unknown to us. Since it is enough for our purpose, let us take for granted that he did not desire more than he had already. Do you think that he was in want?'

Licentius answered: 'Even if I concede that he did not desire anything further—something hard to believe of a man who is not wise—yet, assuredly, he must have been afraid of losing all his possessions through one sudden mishap, since, as it is said, he was a man of high intelligence. For it was not difficult to comprehend that all such things, no matter how great, were subject to chance.'

At this point I smiled and said: 'Lincentius, you see that the brilliancy of his own mind impeded this man, exceptionally favored by fortune, from enjoying the happy life. Through the greater sharpness of his mind he gained a deeper realization of the contingency of his possessions. Therefore he was bent down by fear, and expressed this sufficiently by a common saying; the man without faith is prudent in his own folly.'

When he and the others had smiled, I said: 'Let us consider this a little more carefully, since he (Orata), though imbued with fear, was not in want; from which point rises our question. For, to be in want consists in not possessing, not in fearing the loss of your possessions. He was miserable because of fear, not because of want. Consequently, not everybody is in want who is miserable.'

With all the others, my mother also, whose opinion I was defending, approved of this. Still a little in doubt, she said: 'I do not yet quite understand how misery can be separated from want, and want from misery. Although he had great riches and abundance and—according to your own statement—desired nothing more, he was still in want of wisdom, since he entertained the fear of losing these things. Are we going to consider him in want, if he is without silver and money, and not if he should lack wisdom?'

When, at this point, all had expressed their admiration, and I myself was filled with joy and delight because it was she who had uttered that truth which, as gleaned from the books of the philosophers, I had intended to bring forward as an imposing final argument, I said: 'Do you all see that a great difference exists between many and varied doctrines and a soul that is devoted to God? For from what other sources flow these words that we admire?'

Licentius joyfully exclaimed: 'Verily, no truer or more divine words could have been spoken. For, there is no greater and more pitiable want than the want of wisdom. Whoever does not lack wisdom cannot lack anything.'

'Consequently, the want of the soul is nothing but foolishness,' I said. 'It is the opposite of wisdom, as death is the opposite of life, or a happy life is the opposite of a miserable one, that is, without a middle state. For, just as every man who is not happy is miserable, and everyman who is not dead is alive, so, manifestly, everyman who is not foolish is wise.'

'From this we may rightly conclude that Sergius Orata was miserable, not merely because he feared losing those gifts of fortune, but because he was unwise. Of course, he would have been more miserable if he had been quite without fear for those unsteady and changeable things which he regarded as good. In this case he would have found an added security, not through a watch kept by courage but through a mental lethargy, and his deeper folly would have sunk him deeper into misery. Therefore, if everybody without wisdom suffers from a great want, it follows that foolishness is nothing but want. Just as every fool is miserable, so every miserable man is a fool. Thus, evidently, just as all want is identical with misery, so all misery is identical with want.'

When Trygetius said that he had not satisfactorily grasped this conclusion, I asked: 'Upon what did we agree through logical reasoning?'

'That a person is in want who does not possess wisdom,' he answered.

'What, then, does it mean: to be in want?' I asked.

'Not to possess wisdom,' he answered.

'But, what does it mean: not to possess wisdom?' I said. When he kept silent, I continued: 'Is it not to possess foolishness?'

'Yes,' he answered.

'To have want, then, is nothing but to have foolishness,' I said; 'consequently "want" must be merely another word for "foolishness," although I am unable to explain how we shall say: "He has want, or he has foolishness."

'It is as though, when speaking of a place that

has no light, we were to say that it has darkness, intending only to state that it has no light. For the darkness does not, as it were, come or go away; but to be without light is the same as to be dark, as to be without clothing is the same as to be naked. For, nakedness does not depart, like something moveable, upon the arrival of clothing. Thus, then, we say that someone has want, as we would say that he has nakedness.'

'The expression "want" is a word for "not having." Therefore—to explain what I mean as well as I can—we say "he has want," as though we said "he has not-having." If it is demonstrated that foolishness is really and undoubtedly identical with want, please consider whether the question that we have asked is solved. For, some of us were still in doubt whether what we call misery is nothing but what we call want. But now we have given a reason why foolishness may correctly be called want. Since, therefore, every fool is a miserable, and every miserable person is foolish, we must acknowledge that every person in want is miserable, and also that every miserable person is in want. However, if from the proposition, every fool is miserable and every miserable person is foolish, the conclusion must be that foolishness is identical with misery, why do we not from the proposition, every person in want is miserable and every miserable person is in want, conclude that misery is nothing but want?'

All agreed to this conclusion, and I said: 'Now we have to inquire who it is that is not in want, for it is that person who will be wise and happy. Now, foolishness is want and a term of want, while this word "want" usually signifies a sort of sterility and lack. Kindly pay close attention to the great care with which the ancients have created either all or, as is evident, some words, especially designating those things the knowledge of which was very necessary.'

'You now agree that every fool is in want, and that every person in want is a fool. And I think you also concede that a foolish soul is faulty, and that all faults of the mind can be included in that one term foolishness.'

'On the first day of our discussion we said that the term *nequitia* (worthlessness) is so called because it comes from "not anything," while it's opposite, *frugalitas* (frugality) comes from *frux* (fruit). Therefore, in those two opposites, frugality and worthlessness, two things seem to be evident, namely, *esse* (to be) and *non esse* (not to be). Of what, then, do we conceive as the opposite of "want," about which we are speaking?'

While the others hesitated, Trygetius said: 'If I speak of wealth, I see that poverty is the opposite.'

'This is almost right,' I answered. 'For poverty and want are usually understood in the same sense. But, another word has to be found so that the commendable side may not lack a term. Otherwise, the one side would have two terms (poverty and want) confronted on the other side by the one term (wealth). For, nothing could be more absurd than to lack a word where one is needed in opposition to "want."'

Lincentius said: 'If we may say so, the word "fullness" (*plenitude*) seems to me to be the proper opposite of "want."'

'Perhaps,' I said, 'we will inquire later about this word a little more carefully. For this is not important for the quest of truth. Although Sallust, (that most excellent weigher of words), has chosen "opulence" as the opposite of "want," I accept your "fullness." Here we will not labor in dread of the grammarians, nor will we fear that, for a careless use of words, we will be chastised by those who have permitted us to use their property.'

When they smilingly had given their approval, I said: 'While your thoughts are directed toward God, since I did not intend to disregard your minds, as oracles, so to speak, let us examine the meaning of this term, for I think no term is more adapted to the truth. "Fullness" and "want," then, are opposites. As in the case of "worthlessness" and "frugality," here, too, appear the concepts "to be" and "not to be."

'If "want" is identical with "foolishness," "fullness" will be "wisdom." And, quite correctly, many have called frugality the mother of all virtues.

Tullius also agrees with them, when, in one of his popular orations, he says:

> *"Whatever may be others' opinion, I think that frugality, that is, moderation and restraint, is the greatest virtue."*

This is very learnedly and becomingly said, for he considered the fruit, that is, what we call "to be," whose contrary is "not to be." But, because of the common manner of speech, according to which "frugality" means the same as "thriftiness," he illustrates what he has in mind by adding "moderation" and restraint." Let us now consider these two words more closely.'

'The word *modestia* (moderation) is derived from *modus* (measure), and the word *tempererantia* (restraint) from *temperies* (proper mixture). Wherever measure and proper mixture are, there is nothing either too much or too little. Here, then, we have the precise sense of "fullness" (*plenitude*), which is the word we chose as the opposite of "want" (*egestas*), and more suitably than if we were to use "abundance" (*abundantia*). For, by "abundance" is understood a profusion and a sort of pouring forth of something excessively plentiful.'

'If this happens in excess, there, also, measure is lacking, and the thing that is in excess stands in want of measure. What, then, is not alien even to excess, but both "the more" and "the less" are alien to measure. If you discuss opulence, you will find that it also contains measure, for the word *opulentia* has no other derivation than from *ops* (wealth). But, how does that enrich which is too much, since this is often more inconvenient than too little? Therefore, whatever is either too little or too much is subject to want, since it is in want of measure.

'But the measure of the soul is wisdom. Wisdom, however, is undeniably the opposite of foolishness, and foolishness is want, but fullness the opposite of want. Therefore, wisdom is fullness. Yet, in fullness is measure. Hence, the measure of the soul is in wisdom. Hence, the very famous proverb rightly known as the most useful principle in life: "Not anything too much."'

'At the beginning of our discussion today we intended to call that man happy who is not in want, in case we should find misery identical with want. This is now found to be so. Therefore, "to be happy" means nothing else than "not to be in want," that is, "to be wise."'

'If now you ask what wisdom is—our reason has also explained and developed this as far as was at present possible—the answer is that wisdom is nothing but the measure of the soul, that is, that through which the soul keeps in equilibrium so that it neither runs over into too much nor remains short of its fullness. It runs over into luxuries, despotism, pride, and other things of this kind, through which the souls of immoderate and miserable men believe they get joy and might. But it is narrowed down by meanness, fear, grief, passion, and many other things through which miserable men make acknowledgement of their misery.'

'However, when it (the soul) beholds the wisdom found and, to use the words of the boy here, devotes itself to it, and, without being moved by mere empty vanity, is not seduced to the treachery of images, weighed down in whose embrace it generally deserts God and finds a pernicious end, it then fears no immoderateness, and therefore no want and hence no misery. Thus, whoever is happy possesses his measure, that is, wisdom.'

'But what wisdom should be so called, if not the wisdom of God? We have also heard through divine authority that the Son of God is nothing but the wisdom of God, and the Son of God is truly God. Thus, everyone having God is happy—a statement already acclaimed by everyone at the beginning of our symposium. But, do you believe that wisdom is different from truth? For it has also been said: "I am the Truth." The truth, however, receives its being through a supreme measure, from which it emanates and into which it is converted when perfected. However, no other measure is imposed upon the supreme measure. For, if the supreme measure exists through the supreme measure, it is measure through itself.'

'Of course, the supreme measure must also be a true measure. But, just as the truth is engendered through measure, so measure is recognized in truth. Thus, neither has truth ever been without measure, nor measure without truth.'[vi]

THE HEBREW MORAL DEVELOPMENT
by John Dewey

The interaction between the religious and the moral education of the Hebrews was so intimate that it is difficult to distinguish the two, but we may abstract certain conceptions or motives which were especially significant. The general conception was that of the close personal relation between god and people. Israel should have no other god; Jehovah would have no other people. He had loved and chosen Israel; Israel in gratitude, as well as in hope and fear, must love and obey Jehovah. Prophets brought new commands according to the requirements of the hour; the king represented his sovereignty and justice; the course of events exhibited his purpose. Each of these elements served to elicit moral reflection or moral conduct.

The "Covenant" Relation was a Moral Conception

The usual religious conception is that of some blood or kin relation between people and deity. This has the same potential meaning and value as that of the other relations of group life outlined in Chapter II. But it is rather a natural than a "moral"-- i.e., conscious and voluntary--tie. To conceive of the relation between god and people as due to voluntary choice, is to introduce a powerful agency toward making morality conscious.

Whatever the origin of the idea, the significant fact is that the religious and moral leaders present the relation of Israel to Jehovah as based on a covenant. On the one hand, Jehovah protects, preserves, and prospers; on the other, Israel is to obey his laws and serve no other gods. This conception of mutual obligation is presented at the opening of the "Ten Commandments," and to this covenant relation the prophets again and again make appeal. The obligation to obey the law is not "This is the custom," or "Our fathers did so"; it is placed on the ground that the people has voluntarily accepted Jehovah as its god and lawgiver.

The meaning of this covenant and the symbols by which it was conceived, changed with the advance of the social relationships of the people. At first Jehovah was "Lord of Hosts," protector in war, and giver of prosperity, and the early conceptions of the duty of the people seemed to include human sacrifice, at least in extreme cases. But with later prophets we find the social and family relationship of husband and father brought increasingly into use. Whether by personal experience or by more general reflection, we find Hosea interpreting the relationship between God and his people in both of these family conceptions. The disloyalty of the people takes on the more intimate taint of a wife's unfaithfulness, and, conversely, in contrast to the concepts of other religions, the people may call

Jehovah "my husband" and no longer "my master" (Baal). The change from status to contract is thus, in Israel's religion, fruitful with many moral results.

The Conception of a Personal Lawgiver

The conception of a personal lawgiver raises conduct from the level of custom to the level of conscious morality. So long as a child follows certain ways by imitation or suggestion, he does not necessarily attach any moral meaning to them. But if the parent expressly commands or prohibits, it becomes a matter of obedience or disobedience. Choice becomes necessary. Character takes the place of innocence. Jehovah's law compelled obedience or rebellion. Customs were either forbidden or enjoined. In either case they ceased to be merely customs. In the law of Israel the whole body of observances is introduced with a "Thus says the Lord." We know that other Semitic people observed the Sabbath, practiced circumcision, distinguished clean from unclean beasts, and respected the taboos of birth and death. Whether in Israel all these observances were old customs given new authority by statute, or were customs taken from other peoples under the authority of the laws of Jehovah, is immaterial. The ethical significance of the law is that these various observances, instead of being treated merely as customs, are regarded as personal commands of a personal deity.

This makes a vital difference in the view taken of the violation of these observances. When a man violates a custom he fails to do the correct thing. He misses the mark. But when the observance is a personal command, its violation is a personal disobedience; it is rebellion; it is an act of the will. The evil which follows is no longer bad luck; it is punishment. Now punishment must be either right or wrong, moral or immoral. Hence the very conception of sin as a personal offense, and of ill as a personal punishment, forces a moral standard. In its crudest form this may take the god's commands as right simply because he utters them, and assume that the sufferer is guilty merely because he suffers. We find this in the penitential psalms of the Babylonians. These express the deepest conviction of sin and the utmost desire to please the god, but when we try to discover what the penitent has done that wakens such remorse within him, we find that he seems merely to feel that in some way he has failed to please God, no matter how. He experiences misfortune, whether of disease, or ill-luck, or defeat, and is sure that this must be due to some offense. He does not know what this may be. It may have been that he has failed to repeat a formula in the right manner; it is all one. He feels guilty and even exaggerates his own guilt in view of the punishment which has befallen him. Job's three friends apply the same logic to his case.

But side by side with the conception that the laws of Jehovah must be obeyed because they were his commands, there was another doctrine which was but an extension of the theory that the people had freely accepted their ruler. This was that Jehovah's commands were not arbitrary. They were right; they could be placed before the people for their approval; they were "life"; "the judge of all the earth" would "do right." We have here a striking illustration of the principle that moral standards, at first embodied in persons, slowly work free, so that persons are judged by them.

The Prophets as a Moral Force

The prophets were by far the most significant moral agency in Israel's religion. In the first place, they came to the people bearing a message from a living source of authority, intended for the immediate situation. They brought a present command for a present duty. "Thou art the man," of Nathan to David, "Hast thou killed, and also taken possession?" of Elijah to Ahab, had personal occasions. But the great sermons of Amos, Isaiah, Jeremiah, were no less for the hour. A licentious festival, an Assyrian invasion, an Egyptian embassy, a plague of locusts, and an impending captivity— these inspire demand for repentance, warnings of destruction, and promises of salvation. The prophet was thus the "living fountain." The divine will as coming through him "was still, so to speak, fluid, and not congealed into institutions."

In the second place, the prophets seized upon the inward purpose and social conduct of man as the all-important issues; cultus, sacrifice, are unimportant. "I hate, I despise your feasts, and I will take no delight in your solemn assemblies," cries Amos in Jehovah's name, "But let justice roll down as waters and righteousness as a mighty stream." "I have had enough of the burnt offerings of rams, and the fat of fed beasts," proclaims Isaiah, "new moons, and Sabbaths, the calling of assemblies,--I cannot away with iniquity and the solemn meeting." You need not ceremonial, but moral, purity. "Wash you, make you clean; put away the evil of your doings;--seek justice, relieve the oppressed, judge the fatherless, plead for the widow." Micah's "Shall I give my first-born for my transgression, the fruit of my body for the sin of my soul?" seized upon the difference once for all between the physical and the moral; a completely ethical standpoint is gained in his summary of religious duty: "What does God require of you, but to do justly, and to love mercy, and to walk humbly with your God?" And the New Testament analogue marks the true ethical valuation of all the external religious manifestations, even of the cruder forms of prophecy itself. Gifts, mysteries, knowledge, or the "body to be burned"--there is a more excellent way than these. For all these are "in part." Their value is but temporary and relative. The values that abide, that stand criticism, are that staking of oneself upon the truth and worth of one's ideal which is faith; that aspiration and forward look which is hope; that sum of all charity, sympathy, justice, and active helpfulness, which is love. "But the greatest of these is love."

Religion and the Problem of Evil

The Greek treatment of the problem of evil is found in its great tragedies. An ancestral curse follows down successive generations, dealing woe to the unhappy house. For the victims there seems to be nothing but to suffer. The necessity of destiny makes the catastrophe sublime, but also hopeless. Ibsen's Ghosts is conceived in a similar spirit. There is a tremendous moral lesson in it for the fathers, but for the children only horror. The Greek and the Scandinavian are doubtless interpreting one phase of human life--its continuity and dependence upon cosmic nature. But the Hebrew was not content with this. His confidence in a divine government of the world forced him to seek some moral value, some purpose in the event. The search led in one hand to a readjustment of values; and in another to a new view of social interdependence.

The book of Job gives the deepest study of the

first of these problems. The old view had been that virtue and happiness always went together. Prosperity meant divine favor, and therefore it must be the good. Adversity meant divine punishment; it showed wrongdoing and was itself an evil. When calamity comes upon Job, his friends assume it to be a sure proof of his wickedness. He had himself held the same view, and since he refuses to admit his wickedness and "holds fast to his integrity," it confounds all his philosophy of life and of God. It compels a "reversal and revaluation of all values." If he could only meet God face to face and have it out with him he believes there would be some solution. But come what may, he will not sell his soul for happiness. To "repent," as his friends urge, in order that he may be again on good terms with God, would mean for him to call sin what he believes to be righteousness. And he will not lie in this way. God is doubtless stronger, and if he pursues his victim relentlessly, may convict him. But be this as it may, Job will not let go his fundamental consciousness of right and wrong. His "moral self" is the one anchor that holds, is the supreme value of life.

> *As God lives, who has taken away my right,*
> *And the Almighty, who has embittered my soul,*
> *For as long as life is in me,*
> *And the breath of God is in my nostrils,*

My lips certainly will not speak unjustly,
Nor will my tongue mutter deceit.
Far be it from me that I should declare you right;
Till I die I will not put away my integrity from me.
I hold fast my righteousness and will not let it go.

Job 27:2-6

Another suggestion of the book is that evil comes to prove man's sincerity: "Does Job serve God for naught?" and from that standpoint the answer is, yes; he does. "There is a disinterested love of God." In this setting, also, the experience of suffering produces a shifting of values from the extrinsic to the internal.

The other treatment of the problem of suffering is found in the latter half of Isaiah. It finds an interpretation of the problem by a deeper view of social interdependence, in which the old tribal solidarity is given, as it were, a transfigured meaning. The individualistic interpretation of suffering was that it meant personal guilt. "We did esteem him stricken of God." This breaks down. The suffering servant is not wicked. He is suffering for others--in some sense. "He has borne our grief and carried our sorrow." The conception here reached of an interrelation which involves that the suffering of the good may be due to the sin or the suffering of others, and that the assumption of this burden marks the higher type of ethical relation, is one of the finest products of Israel's religion. As made central in the Christian conception of the Cross, it has furnished one of the great elements in the modern social consciousness.[vii]

THE ETHICS OF CONFUCIUS
by Miles Dawson

What Constitutes The Superior Man

The central idea of Confucius is that every human being cherishes the aspiration to become a superior man—superior to his fellows, if possible, but surely superior to his own past and present self. This does not more than hint at perfection as a goal; and it is said of him that one of the subjects concerning which the Master rarely spoke, was "perfect virtue." He also said, "They who know virtue, are few," and was far from teaching a perfectionist doctrine. It refers rather to the perpetually relative, the condition of being superior to that to which one may be superior, be it high or low,—that hopeful possibility which has ever lured mankind toward higher things. The aim to excel, if respected of all, approved and accepted by common consent, would appeal to every child and, logically presented to its mind and enforced by universal recognition of its validity, would become a conviction and a scheme for the art of living, of transforming power and compelling vigor. In various sayings Confucius, his disciples, and Mencius present the attributes of the superior man, whom the sage adjures his disciples to admire without ceasing, to emulate without turning, and to imitate without hindrance. These are some of them:

Purpose: "The superior man learns in order to attain to the utmost of his principles" (Analects, bk. xix., c. vii).

Poise: "The superior man in his thought does not go out of his place" (Analects, bk. xiv., c. xxviii).

Self-sufficiency: "What the superior man seeks is in himself; what the ordinary man seeks, is in others" (Analects, bk. xv., c. xx).

Earnestness: "The superior man in everything puts forth his utmost endeavors" (Great Learning, ii., 4).

Thoroughness: "The superior man bends his attention to what is radical. That being established, all practical courses naturally grow up"(Analects, bk. i., c. ii., v. 2).

Sincerity: "The superior man must make his thoughts sincere" (Great Learning, vi.,4). "Is it not his absolute sincerity which distinguishes a superior man?" (Doctrine of the Mean, c. xiii., 4).

Truthfulness: "What the superior man requires is that in what he says there may be nothing inaccurate" (Analects, bk. xiii., c. iii., v. 7).

Purity of thought and action: "The superior man must be watchful over himself when alone" (Great Learning, vi., 2).

Love of truth: "The object of the superior man is truth" (Analects, bk. xv., c. xxxi). "The superior man is anxious lest he should not get truth; he is not anxious lest poverty come upon him" (Analects, bk. xv., c. xxxi).

Mental hospitality: "The superior man is catholic and not partisan; the ordinary man is partisan and not catholic" (Analects, bk. ii., c. xiv). "The superior man in the world does not set his mind either for anything or against anything; what is right, he will follow" (Analects, bk. iv., c. x).

Rectitude: "The superior man thinks of virtue; the ordinary man thinks of comfort" (Analects, bk. iv., c. xi). "The mind of the superior man is conversant with righteousness; the mind of the ordinary man is conversant with gain" (Analects, bk. iv., c. xxi). "The superior man in all things considers righteousness essential" (Analects, bk. xv., c. xvii).

Prudence: "The superior man wishes to be slow in his words and earnest in his conduct" (Analects, bk. iv., c. xxiv).

Composure: "The superior man is satisfied and composed; the ordinary man is always full of distress" (Analects, bk. vii., c. xxxvi). "The superior man may indeed have to endure want; but the ordinary man, when he is in want, gives way to unbridled license" (Analects, bk. xv., c. i., v. 3).

Fearlessness: "The superior man has neither anxiety nor fear" (Analects, bk. xii., c. iv., v. 1). "When internal examination discovers nothing wrong, what is there to be anxious about, what is there to fear?" (Analects, bk. xi., c. iv., v. 3). "They sought to act virtuously and they did so; and what was there for them to repine about?" (Analects, bk. vii., c. xiv., v. 2).

Ease and dignity: "The superior man has dignified ease without pride; the ordinary man has pride without dignified ease" (Analects, bk. xiii., c. xxvi). "The superior man is dignified and does not wrangle" (Analects, bk. xv., c. xxi).

Firmness: "Refusing to surrender their wills or to submit to any taint to their persons" (Analects, bk. xviii., c. viii., v. 2). "The superior man is correctly firm and not merely firm" (Analects, bk. xv., c. xxxvi). "Looked at from a distance, he appears stern; when approached, he is mild; when he is heard to speak, his language is firm and decided."

Lowliness: "The superior man is affable but not adulatory; the ordinary man is adulatory but not affable" (Analects, bk. xiii., c. xxiii).

Avoidance of sycophancy: "I have heard that the superior man helps the distressed, but he does not add to the wealth of the rich"(Analects, bk. vi., c. iii., v. 2).

Growth: "The progress of the superior man is upward, the progress of the ordinary man is downward" (Analects, bk. xiv., c. xxiv). "The superior man is distressed by his want of ability; he is not distressed by men's not knowing him" (Analects, bk. xv., c. xviii).

Capacity: "The superior man cannot be known in little matters but may be entrusted with great concerns" (Analects, bk. xv., c. xxxiii).

Openness: "The faults of the superior man are like the sun and moon. He has his faults and all men see them. He changes again and all men look up to him" (Analects, bk. xix., c. xxi).

Benevolence: "The superior man seeks to develop the admirable qualities of men and does not seek to develop their evil qualities. The ordinary man does the opposite of this" (Analects, bk. xii., c. xvi).

Broadmindedness: "The superior man honors talent and virtue and bears with all. He praises the good and pities the incompetent" (Analects, bk. xix., c. iii). "The superior man does not promote a man on account of his words, nor does he put aside good words on account of the man" (Analects, bk. xv., c. xxii).

Charity: "To be able to judge others by what is in ourselves, this may be called the art of virtue" (Analects, bk. vi., c. xxviii., v. 3).

Moderation: "The superior man conforms with the path of the Mean" (Doctrine of the mean, c. xi., v. 3).

The [Silver] Rule: "When one cultivates to the utmost the capabilities of his nature and exercises them on the principle of reciprocity, he is not far from the path. What you do not want done to yourself, do not do unto others" (Doctrine of the Mean, c. xiii., v. 3).

Reserve power: "That wherein the superior man cannot be equaled is simply this, his work which other men cannot see" (Doctrine of the Mean, cxxxiii., v. 2).

The Art of Living. "The practice of right-living is deemed the highest, the practice of any other art lower. Complete virtue takes first place; the doing of anything else whatsoever is subordinate" (Li Ki, bk. xvii., sect. iii., 5).

Self-Development

The characteristics of the superior man having been presented, it is in logical order to examine the faculties and qualities which Confucius would have one cultivate to attain this ideal state. First in importance is the will. The Will. "Their purposes being rectified, they cultivated themselves." By these words in "The Great Learning" (Text, v. 5) it is meant that when there is no conflict of aims, of duties and desires, when one wills what he wishes, and with all his heart singly and clearly wishes what he wills, then and not till then does the will become clear and firm and strong. The man is his will; back of his will is his purpose; and back of his purpose, his desire. If his knowledge enable him to make right choices, he should be sincere, his desires should be disciplined, his purpose lofty, and, resting thereupon as on a rock, his will fixed and immovable. That is character. Confucius puts it: "If the will be set on virtue, there will be no practice of wickedness" (Analects, bk. iv., c. iv). True; for when the will rests upon set purpose, based upon purified desire, born of knowledge and discriminating investigation of phenomena, nothing can undermine it! This rectification of the antecedent conditions is what the sage refers to when he says: "To subdue one's self and return to propriety is perfect virtue" (Analects, bk. xii., c. 1), and again: "The firm, the enduring, the simple, and the unpretentious are near to virtue" (Analects, bk. xiii., c. xxvii). That the will is proved by its resistance rather than its impelling force, Mencius says in this: "Men must be resolute about what they will not do and then they are able to act with vigor" (Bk. iv., pt. ii., c. viii). The same is meant when Confucius says: "The commander of the forces of a large state may be carried off, but the will of even a common man cannot be taken from him" (Analects, bk. ix., c. xxv).

Confucius refuses to accept the excuse of inability unless one actually expires in a supreme effort to achieve. Therefore, when his disciple, Yen K'ew, said: "It is not that I do not delight in your doctrines, but my strength is insufficient," he admonished him: "They whose strength is insufficient give over in the middle of the way, but now you do but set limits unto yourself" (Analects, bk. vi., c. x). The scorn of craven compromise is well voiced in this: "Tsze-Chang said, 'When a man holds fast virtue, but without seeking to enlarge it, and credits right principles, but without firm sincerity, what account can be made of his existence or nonexistence?" (Analects, bk. xix., c. ii).

That the path of duty leads to the very brink of the grave—and beyond it—Confucius says in no uncertain language: "The determined scholar and the man of virtue will not seek to live at the expense of injuring their virtue. They will even sacrifice their lives to preserve their virtue complete" (Analects, bk. xiv., c. viii). "The man who in the view of gain thinks of righteousness, who in the view of danger is prepared to give up his life, and who does not forget an old agreement, however far back it extends—such a man may be reckoned a complete man" (Analects, bk. xiv., c. xiii., v. 2). His disciple, Tsze-Chang, said of this: "The scholar, beholding threatened danger, is prepared to sacrifice his life. When the opportunity for gain is presented to him, he thinks of righteousness" (Analects, bk. xix., c. i). This picture, which to uninstructed mortals may seem dark and forbidding,—it should not seem so, since to die is before every man and few can hope to have so noble an end,—Confucius did not always hold before the eyes of his disciples, however, but on the contrary justly declared, in the face of their craven dread: "Virtue is more to man than either fire or water. I have seen men die by treading upon fire or water, but I have never seen a man die by treading the path of virtue" (Analects, bk. xv., c. xxxiv). It costs really nothing to will that which is good and beneficial; the cost is all on the other side.

That one sacrifices, is pure delusion; the pleasure as well as the solid benefit is to be found where the enlightened will would bear us. Such conduct is heroic to contemplate; but it is simple truth and not merely personal praise which Confucius spoke of another: "With a single bamboo dish of rice, a single gourd dish of drink, and living in a mean, narrow lane, while others could not have endured the distress, he did not allow his joy to be affected by it" (Analects, bk. vi., c. ix).

It might, indeed it ought and would, be true of any other, if unspoiled; and, as he has well said: "For a morning's anger, to wreck one's life and involve the lives of his parents, is not this a case of delusion?" (Analects, bk. xii., c. xxi., v. 3). And, while not so strikingly and obviously true, this statement holds for every aberration from the path of duty, into which one may believe himself led by reason of the greater pleasure and satisfaction that it seems to offer, be it what it may. The beauty, the compensations and relaxations of the upward course are thus set forth by the sage: "Let the will be set on the path of duty! Let every attainment of what is good be firmly grasped! Let perfect virtue be emulated! Let relaxation and enjoyment be found in the polite arts!" (Analects, bk. vii., c. vi). To the instructed mind there is nothing uninviting in this prospect; and low and mind destroying pleasures and comforts which are in fact, though not apparently, lower and more destructive are well abandoned for these higher, simpler, keener, and more abiding satisfactions.

Confucius puts it also more explicitly thus: "To find enjoyment in the discriminating study of ceremonies and music; to find enjoyment in speaking of the goodness of others; to find enjoyment in having many worthy friends: these are advantageous. To find enjoyment in extravagant pleasures; to find enjoyment in idleness and sauntering; to find enjoyment in the pleasures of feasting: these are injurious" (Analects, bk. xvi., c.).

Even reverses and hardships have their lesson and reward if one but meet them with resolution; for as Mencius says: "When Heaven is about to confer a great office on any man, it first disciplines his mind with suffering and his bones and sinews with toil. It exposes him to want and subjects him to extreme poverty. It confounds his undertakings. By all these methods it stimulates his mind, hardens him, and supplies his shortcomings" (Bk. vi., pt. ii., c. xv., v. 2).

This development of the will, which is the development of the man, is therefore not a thing to terrify or repel. Instead, it is mastery, power, sway, achievement—that for which the mind of man longs unceasingly. And it comes of itself, if the basis for it has been safely and carefully laid in purified desires and righteous aims, without effort, without strain, without pain or penalty. "Is virtue a thing remote?" asked the sage; and answered: "I wish to be virtuous, and lo, virtue is at hand!" (Analects, bk. vii., c. xxix). What, then, is this will? What, this virtue?

The disciples of Confucius handed the secret of it down from one to another, in these words: "The doctrine of our master is to be true to the principles of our nature and the benevolent exercise of them to others" (Analects, bk. iv., c. xv., v. 2). That the joy of well doing is more than comparable with the pleasure of abandonment to sensual playing with elemental appetites, is said in these words of Wu, reported in the "Shu King": "I have heard that the good man, doing good, finds the day insufficient; and that the evil man, doing evil, also finds the day insufficient." (Pt. v., bk. i., sect. 2).

Fortitude. When the will accords completely with the purpose and the desire, courage follows necessarily; for, if one desires a given result, designs to compass it, and wills to achieve it, it can only mean that he is not fearful about it but instead is cool and determined. As it costs nothing to will, when the purposes are rectified; so, when the will is clear and firm, it costs nothing to be brave. Therefore in "The Great Learning" it is said that by this course, "unperturbed resolve is attained." Confucius elsewhere puts it: "To see what is right and not to do it, is want of courage" (Analects, bk.

ii., c.xxiv., v. 2). For if one see what is right, he
should think sincerely about it, without self-
delusion; and, thinking thus, his desires and his
purposes should be rectified and there will to do
right will flow. And if he see the truth and does not
do these things, it is plainly want of courage—the
courage to cast aside comfortable delusions, to
think sincerely and be undeceived. When
undeceived and with desire and resolve purified, the
will and courage follow inevitably. Confucius again
refers to this, saying: "When you have faults, do not
fear to abandon them" (Analects, bk. i., c. viii., v. 4).
This is also the gist of the following injunction from
the "Li Ki:" "Do not try to defend or conceal what
was wrong in the past" (bk. xv., v. 22).

The fear here referred to is doubtless both the
fear of discomfort and the fear of the prying eyes
and the caustic tongues of others. To this craven
dread, reference is made when Tsze-Hea says: "The
inferior man is sure to gloss his faults" (Analects,
bk. xix., c. viii). The remedy for it, Confucius
demonstrates in these brave words: "I am fortunate!
If I have any faults, people are sure to know them"
(Analects, bk. vii., c. xxx., v. 3). Thus Mencius puts
it: "When any one told Tsze-loo that he had a fault,
he rejoiced" (Bk. ii., pt. i., c. viii., v. 1).

Fearlessness Confucius ever named as an
attribute of the superior man, saying: "The way of
the superior man is threefold, but I am not equal to

it. Virtuous, he is free from anxieties; wise, he is free from perplexities; bold, he is free from fear" (Analects, bk. xiv., c. xxx., v. 1). He also presents this opposite picture: "They who are without virtue cannot abide long either in a condition of poverty and hardship or in a condition of enjoyment" (Analects, bk. iv., c. ii). This is even more strikingly presented in the following: "Having not and yet affecting to have, empty and yet affecting to be full, straitened and yet affecting to be at ease! It is difficult with such characteristics to have constancy" (Analects, bk. vii., c. xxv., v.3). And in this contrast: "The superior man is satisfied and composed, the ordinary man is always full of distress" (Analects, bk. vii., c. xxxvi).

That the bravery of the superior man and the bravado of the inferior should be distinguished, is the gist of the following saying: "Men of principle are sure to be bold, but those who are bold may not always be men of principle" (Analects, bk. xiv., c. v). The absolute need of fearlessness, Mencius enjoins in this which he puts into the mouth of Mang She-Shay: "I look upon not conquering and conquering in the same way. To measure the enemy and then advance, to calculate the chances of victory and then engage—this is to stand in dread of the opposing force. How can I make certain of conquering? But I can rise superior to all fear" (Bk. ii., pt. i., c. ii., v. 5).

The shame of moral cowardice is well set forth by Confucius in the "Yi King," thus: "If one be distressed by what need not distress him, his name is sure to be disgraced" (Appendix iii., sect. ii., c. v). What, then, may the superior man fear? The answer, disclosing that upon which the courage of the superior man rests securely, is in this query: "They sought to act virtuously and they did so; and what was there for them to repine about?" (Analects, bk. vii., c. xiv., v. 2). The freedom from fear which is here referred to costs no effort; if the precedent conditions have been fulfilled, it is their natural and necessary consequence and appears in the noble attributes of the superior man, to which Confucius often adverted, as thus: "The superior man has neither anxiety nor fear" (Analects, bk. xii, c. iv., v. 1). "When internal examination discovers nothing wrong, what is there to be anxious about, what is there to fear?" (Analects, bk. xii., c. iv., v. 3).

Thus the sage has said: "What the superior man seeks, is in himself; what the ordinary man seeks, is in others" (Analects, bk. xiv., c. xxviii). In the "Yi King" (appendix ii., c. iii.), it is put thus: "The superior man does not in his thoughts go beyond the position in which he is." And thus, also: "The influence of the world would make no change in him; he would do nothing merely to secure fame. He can live withdrawn from the world without regret; he can experience disapproval without a troubled mind... He is not to be torn from his root." (Appendix iv., c. ii., v. 41). In the "Li Ki" this is much expatiated upon, in part only as follows: "The scholar keeps himself free from all stain; . . . he does not go among those who are low, to make himself seem high, nor set himself among those who are foolish, to make himself seem wise; . . . he does not approve those who think as he, nor condemn those who think differently; thus he takes his stand alone and pursues his course, unattended" (Bk. xxxviii., v. 15).

How this singleness of purpose and this perfect poise of soul, unsuspected during an uneventful life, when great occasion arises, stand forth and reveal the man, is the burden of this saying: "The superior man cannot be known in little matters but he may be entrusted with great concerns" (Analects, bk. xv., c. xxxiii). Self-Control. "Want of forbearance in small matters confounds great plans" (Analects, bk. xv., c. xxvi).

The need for constancy and self-control is often urged by the sage, as thus: "Inconstant in his virtue, he will be visited with disgrace" (Analects, bk. xiii., c. xxii., v. 2). In the "Shu King," I Yin is represented as expressing this sentiment: "Be careful to strive after the virtue of self-restraint and to cherish far-reaching plans" (Pt. iv., bk. v., sect. 1, 2).

What is emphasized in these passages, is that he who has formed worthy conceptions of the significance of life and correct designs for accomplishing its ends must not permit himself, at unguarded moments, to be surprised into revelations of deeper seated longings, by the unexpected presentation of opportunities for the safe enjoyment of sensual delights or by the excitement of rage or terror or other unworthy emotion. It is well said in the "Shi King" (Minor Odes of the Kingdom, decade v., ode 2): "Men who are grave and wise, though they drink, are masters of themselves. While men who are benighted and ignorant become slaves of drink. Be careful, each of you, of your conduct! What Heaven confers, when once lost, will not be regained."

The necessity for reflection and consideration, though it be but momentary, before responding to any impulse from without, either in speech or in action, instead of the automatic, animal response of a curse or a blow, a smile or a caress, or whatever it may be when one is played upon, is always present in the mind of the sage. That even greater prudence in speech is desirable, is indicated by this reply to the inquiry of Tsze-kung: "What constitutes the superior man?" "He acts before he speaks and afterwards speaks in accordance with his act" (Analects, bk. ii., c. xiii).

Reasons for reticence are given in several passages, from which these are culled: "The Master said, 'The superior man is modest in his speech but exceeds in his actions' " (Analects, bk. xiv., c. xxix). "This man seldom speaks; when he does, he is sure to hit the point" (Analects, bk. xi., c. xiii., v. 3). "When a man feels the difficulty of doing, can he be otherwise than cautious and slow in speaking?" (Analects, bk. xii., c. iii., v.3). "The reason why the ancients did not readily give utterance to their words was because they feared lest their deeds should not come up to them." (Analects, bk. iv., c. xxii). The prudence of this course is illustrated in the "Shi King" (Major Odes, decade iii., ode 2) by this apt comparison: "A flaw in a mace of white jade may be ground away, but a word spoken amiss cannot be mended."

An entire book, bearing the title: "The Doctrine of the Mean," consisting chiefly of sayings of Confucius upon this subject, survives. The following account of its origin is found in the introduction: "This work contains the law of the mind which was handed down from one to another in the Confucian School till Tsze-Tsze (the grandson of Confucius), fearing lest in the course of time errors should arise about it, committed it to writing and delivered it to Mencius." What is meant by "the mean" is the virtue which the Greeks especially praised under the name of temperance. It is defined in the "Li Ki" as follows: "Pride should not be allowed to grow. The desires should not be indulged. The will should not be gratified to the full. Pleasure should not be carried to excess" (Bk. i., sect. i., pt. i., c. ii).

The difficulty, indeed the well-nigh impossibility, of attaining this perfect self-control was appreciated by Confucius, who often spoke of it, saying: "All men say, 'We are wise;' but happening to choose the path of the mean, they are not able to keep it for a round month" (Doctrine of the Mean, c. vi). And again: "The empire, its states, and its families may be perfectly ruled, dignities and emoluments may be declined, naked weapons may be trampled under the feet, but the course of the mean cannot be attained to" (Doctrine of the Mean, c. ix). And in another place he says: "The good man tries to proceed according to the right path, but when he has gone half-way he abandons it" (Doctrine of the Mean, c. xi., v. 2). Yet he does not overemphasize this nor fail to recognize that this path is as frequently found by the lowly and humble as by those who are conscious of greatness. He says, instead: "The path is not far from man. When men try to pursue a course which is far from the common indications of consciousness, this course cannot be considered the path" (Doctrine of the Mean, c. xiii., v. 1). Mencius in two places reverently echoes this sentiment, as follows: "The path of duty lies in what is near and men seek for it in what is remote; to follow it is easy and men seek it among arduous undertakings" (Bk. iv., pt. i., c. xi). "The way of truth is like a great road. It is not hard to find it. The trouble is only that men will not look for it. Go home and seek it and you will find many ready to point it out" (Bk. vi., pt. ii., c. ii., v.7).

Confucius finds the starting point for following the path of the mean in this, that one should be natural, should be himself. The whole picture of what is fundamentally necessary and of what result may be hoped for is in the following from the "Doctrine of the Mean" (c. xiv.): "The superior man does what is proper to the station in which he is, he does not desire to go beyond this. In a position of wealth and honor he does what is proper to a position of wealth and honor; in a poor and low position, he does what is proper to a poor and low position; situated among barbarous tribes, he does what is proper to a situation among barbarous tribes; in a position of sorrow and difficulty, he does what is proper to a position of sorrow and difficulty. "The superior man can find himself in no position in which he is not himself. In a high situation he does not treat with contempt his inferiors, in a low situation he does not court the favor of his superiors. He rectifies himself, and seeks for nothing from others, so that he has no dissatisfaction. "He does not murmur against

Heaven nor grumble against men. Thus it is that the superior man is quiet and calm, waiting for the appointments of Heaven, while the inferior man walks in dangerous paths, looking for lucky occurrences."[viii]

ETHICAL THEMES IN AVERROES
by John C. Wilhelmsson

Averroes was born in Cordoba, Spain in 1126 A.D. Highly skilled in law, philosophy, theology, medicine, and many other arts Averroes came from a noble family in which both his grandfather and father had served as the Chief Judge of Cordoba.

Averroes was particularly skilled in medicine yet particularly interested in the relationship between theology and philosophy (or faith and reason). Although he has been called a rationalist his position on the search for truth is actually much more subtle. Averroes held that there is no conflict between theology and philosophy and that they are rather just different ways of reaching religious truth. The first being the way of faith and the second being the way of reason. Philosophy, as the higher path, being reserved for those of the learned who have the good fortune to study it. In his work _The Exposition_ he says of this relationship:

> In a separate treatise, we have already dealt with the harmony of philosophy and religion, indicating how religion commands the study of philosophy. We maintained there that religion consists of two parts: external and interpreted, and that the external part is incumbent on the masses, whereas the interpreted is incumbent on the learned.

The separate work referred to here is _The Decisive Treatise_. In it Averroes lays out the proper way for philosophical or logical methods to be used in religious controversies. He starts by defining philosophy as "The investigation of existing entities in so far as they point to the maker." Averroes then goes on to claim that sacred scripture itself calls for the use of philosophy in such interpretation when, in Qur'anic verses such as 59:2, it urges people of understanding to reflect and, in verse 7:184, it asks believers to use reason and intellect. For these reasons, Averroes contends that the claims of some Muslim theologians that philosophy is useless to religion are not only false, but are in fact contrary to sacred scripture itself which in fact calls for the use of such reflective methods of thought.

In this way Averroes begins to show his ability for critical exegesis of Quranic verses. Yet this exegesis is limited both in terms of who is qualified to engage in it and in which scriptures might be interpreted. Averroes holds that statements of scripture that are explicit do not call for any interpretation but that statements of scripture that are ambiguous should be interpreted yet only by the learned. And that the learned should not share these interpretations with the masses but only among their own class.

Averroes holds that there are, in total, three ways of arriving at religious truth, and that philosophy, as the best of these ways, should not be prohibited. In explaining the three ways Averroes points out that any religion which posits a universal acceptance must present its message in a suitable form for all. And that the learned will be attracted to Islam by philosophical arguments, the theologians will be attracted by an understanding of parables, and the common people, who are not capable of such understandings, will be attracted by rhetorical devices which include some logic yet mainly rely upon imagery and exhortation.

Averroes also challenged various versions of Islamic theology noting that certain issues arising out of their notions of occasionalism, divine speech, and explanations of the origin of the world could not be explained in depth without engaging in the critical thinking that only philosophy can bring. He went on to claim that without philosophy deeper meanings of Islam might ultimately be lost leading to many deviant and incorrect understandings of Islamic theology (and he seems to have been quite prophetic in this).

Averroes has also had a tremendous impact on Christianity. This is because Averroes was "The Commentator" on "The Philosopher" himself

Aristotle. And these very terms "The Commentator" and "The Philosopher" were coined by none other than the great Catholic scholar Saint Thomas Aquinas. For much of what Aquinas learned about Aristotle in the thirteenth century is due to the commentaries Averroes wrote on him in the twelfth. The <u>New World Encyclopedia</u> says of Averroes' role in the transmission of Aristotle's thought:

> *Averroes wrote three versions of his commentaries on Aristotle, known as the Minor, the Middle, and the Major commentaries... The Major commentaries were largely original. Averroes' commentaries do not provide a literal translation of Aristotle's works; since Averroes did not know Greek, he used an imperfect Arab translation of the Syriac version of the Greek text. The Commentaries do, however, contain detailed philosophical and scientific interpretations of Aristotle's thought.*

Before 1150 A.D. only a few translated works of Aristotle existed in Europe and they did not receive a great deal of attention from scholars. It was only through the Latin translations of Averroes' works, beginning in the 12th century, that the legacy of Aristotle was recovered in the West by figures like Saint Thomas Aquinas.

Although little is known directly about Averroes' ethical thought we can at least begin to formulate an understanding based on what we do know. Averroes was born into a distinguished family of Malikite lawyers which suggests he must have been well versed in Islamic Law from a young age. He also, like his father and grandfather, rose to the position of Chief Judge of Cordoba and wrote an influential book on Sunnite justice (*Biddyaf Almujiahid*). We can also be sure that he conducted an extensive study of Greek philosophy because of his highly influential commentaries on both Plato's "Republic" and Aristotle's "Nicomachean Ethics." These studies, along with his Greek medical training, must have impressed on him the importance of the health of the soul. Add to this his ongoing clashes with Asharite theology over the nature of ethics and one begins to see that Averroes must have conducted one of the deepest reflections on religion, law, and ethics of his day.

The longest single passage written by him on values and ethics is in his work *"Kitab al-kashf 'an manahij al-'adilla"* (translated into English as <u>Faith & Reason in Islam</u>). In this work the theory of value is concerned with the nature of good and evil in general as applied to aesthetics, morals, and ethics. The primary question is what is the common denominator in everything we think of as "good"?

(which of course then naturally implies the same question about evil). Another way to state the question is to ask what is that particular value we find in all of the things we consider to be good? Averroes often asks these questions in terms of the value of justice.

For Averroes, the foundational question with regard to value is whether it is objective or subjective. Or whether it is something inherent in the thing being valued or just an idea or attitude the one valuing it brings with them to the consideration? His answer is to always strongly assert the objectivist position. That is to state that value is something real and inherent in the thing being valued and not just an opinion or attitude projected onto it by the one judging.

Here we can see an echo of both the thought of Plato and Aristotle. Plato in his insistence on both the *appearance* and *reality* of a thing. Or that just because a person thinks that the shadows and the echoes of the cave are real they are not necessarily so. And Aristotle's theory of substance and accidents in which he speaks of the *essential* and *accidental* properties of a thing. Or that a chair can be made of wood or metal yet this is accidental to its being a chair. To put it in technical terms, an accident is a property which has no necessary connection to the essence of the thing being described. Thus one can see a definite objectivist bent in Classical Greek thought.

In contrast, in the Islamic thought of Averroes' day subjectivism was both quite prevalent and venerable. The roots of this were currents rising out of the assumptions of early Muslim thinkers about the nature of Islam itself. This theological subjectivism quite naturally led to ethical voluntarism. In this sense ethical voluntarism is the theory that good and evil and justice and injustice are defined entirely by reference to the commands of God as understood through some accepted source of divine revelation (in this case the Sharia). Human acts are thus right or wrong only because god commands them and not because of some intrinsic value of the act in question. To put it in a more clear yet, admittedly, colloquial tone this is the attitude, sometimes expressed by practitioners of various different religious faiths, often stated something like: "God said it, I believe it, and that settles it." A sort of a faith without reason.

This theory had been originally stated in Asharite theology and in Averroes' day had recently been strongly restated by al-Ghazali in his work _The Incoherence of the Philosophers_. In a wonderful twist of words Averroes responded to this work with one of his own entitled _The Incoherence of the Incoherence_ in which, in order to create a harmony between faith and reason. he almost line by line attempts to refute al'Ghazali's work

However, Averroes' most explicit writing on good and evil is found in his work _Mandhij_ or _Exposition of the Methods of Doctrine Concerning the Dogmas of Faith_. In a long passage he lays out the critical problem with the Asharite position.

> _Concerning justice and injustice as applied to God and the Glorious, the Asharites have maintained an opinion that is very foreign to reason and scripture… For they have said that the unseen world is different in this respect than the visible world, because they assert, the visible world is characterized by justice and injustice only by reason of a prohibition of religion against certain acts. Thus a man is just when he does something that is just according to the Law, while he is unjust if he does what the Law has laid down as unjust. But they say: 'As for Him (God) who is not under obligation and does not come under the prohibition of the Law, in His case there does not exist any act which is just or unjust, or rather all His acts are just.' And they are forced to say that there is nothing just in itself and nothing unjust in_

itself. This is extremely disgraceful, because in that case there would be nothing that is good (khayr) in itself and nothing that is evil (sharr) in itself; but it is self-evident that justice is good and injustice is evil. (113.7-17).

Here Averroes shows quite plainly the absurdity of voluntarism by pointing out that it allows for the existence of a god who acts, at least according to the law, unjustly and that, since to be just is good and unjust evil, in doing so it allows for a god who, according to the law, is capable of committing evil!

It is important to note that Averroes comments here are not the polemic of an outsider but rather the criticisms of a very well accomplished and respected insider who sat as the Chief Judge of Cordoba and came from a noble Islamic family line. And that the main point here indeed revolves around a defense of the veracity of Islamic Law.

Averroes did not write any formal work on ethics yet he dealt with many ethical themes. Perhaps a good place to start are his thoughts on the age old problem of evil. He begins with a quote from the Quran: "*He leads astray whom He will, and guides whom He will*" (xvi, 95/93). Averroes says of this verse in his work Manahij:

> *[It} refers to an antecedent [divine] Will which requires that there should be among the kinds of beings creatures who go astray, i.e. predisposed to go astray by their natures, and impelled to it by causes of misguidance, both internal and external, which surround them (114.15-17).*

This verse would seem to suggest that God creates certain men who are predisposed toward evil. And indeed this is the intended meaning. However, Averroes wishes this to be understood not in terms of particulars but of species. God has decided to make this man just and this man unjust, however, God does not choose these men individually but only as a certain number of the whole being either just or unjust. In this way Averroes removes any personal intention in God making certain man evil.

What is the good or end of life for an individual human being? Averroes' answer here seems to be that it is happiness. The evidence for this comes from his commentary on Plato's Republic.

> *The kinds of ultimate happiness which are the ends of human virtue are represented [in allegories] by corresponding goods such as are [commonly] supposed to be the ends.*

Notice that Averroes here is equating *"happiness"* with the *"good"* and stating that they will both be a product of *"human virtue."* He further restates this connection by stating the following:

> *Right practice consists in performing the acts which bring happiness and avoiding the acts which bring misery.*

Yet what is this right practice and is it the same for all or does it allow for a certain diversity of thought?

As a faithful adherent to Islam one would expect Averroes to state that religious adherence is the way to ultimate happiness. And he in fact does do this. However, it is not without qualification:

> *In short, the religions are, according to the philosophers obligatory, since they lead toward wisdom in a way universal to all human beings, for philosophy only leads a certain number of intelligent people to the knowledge of happiness and they therefore have to learn wisdom, whereas religions seek the instruction of the masses generally.*

The modern thinker should be cautioned to not read into this a certain classism or stratification of society, but rather to realize the implications of such a thought with regard to the issue of voluntarism.

For a religion to be something knowable by a purely intellectual means would require that it is in some way reasonable. For to say that a religion can be known purely by reason is to say, in fact, that one's faith is reasonable. And to say that one's faith is reasonable is in fact to say that one's God is not voluntarist in nature but instead somehow bound by a greater sense of reason and morality.

In fact, what Averroes is pointing to here should be very familiar to many of those reading this book. For he is pointing to a place outside of traditional religion where people with special intellectual gifts can pursue wisdom. A place which does not just exist for itself but exists so that the rest of society might be made better through this pursuit of wisdom. And what could this place be but something very much like a university? Thus we begin to see how Averroes is not only celebrated as a great Islamic scholar, but as one of the founders of modern secular European thought as well. [ix]

SUMMA THEOLOGICA

by Thomas Aquinas

Whether human virtue is a habit? (55)

Objection 1: It would seem that human virtue is not a habit: For virtue is "the limit of power" (De Coelo i, text. 116). But the limit of anything is reducible to the genus of that of which it is the limit; as a point is reducible to the genus of line. Therefore virtue is reducible to the genus of power and not to the genus of habit.

Objection 2: Further, Augustine says (De Lib. Arb. ii) [*Retract. ix; cf. De Lib. Arb. ii, 19] that "virtue is good use of free-will." But use of free-will is an act. Therefore virtue is not a habit, but an act.

Objection 3: Further, we do not merit by our habits, but by our actions: otherwise a man would merit continually, even while asleep. But we do merit by our virtues. Therefore virtues are not habits, but acts.

Objection 4: Further, Augustine says (De Moribus Eccl. xv) that "virtue is the order of love," and (QQ. lxxxiii, qu. 30) that "the ordering which is called virtue consists in enjoying what we ought to enjoy, and using what we ought to use." Now order, or ordering, denominates either an action or a relation.

Therefore virtue is not a habit, but an action or a relation.

Objection 5: Further, just as there are human virtues, so are there natural virtues. But natural virtues are not habits, but powers. Neither therefore are human virtues habits.

On the Contrary: The Philosopher says (Category. vi) that science and virtue are habits.

I Answer That: Virtue denotes a certain perfection of a power. Now a thing's perfection is considered chiefly in regard to its end. But the end of power is act. Wherefore power is said to be perfect, according as it is determinate to its act. Now there are some powers which of themselves are determinate to their acts; for instance, the active natural powers. And therefore these natural powers are in themselves called virtues. But the rational powers, which are proper to man, are not determinate to one particular action, but are inclined indifferently to many: and they are determinate to acts by means of habits, as is clear from what we have said above (Q[49], A[4]). Therefore human virtues are habits.

Reply to Objection 1: Sometimes we give the name of a virtue to that to which the virtue is directed, namely, either to its object, or to its act:

for instance, we give the name Faith, to that which we believe, or to the act of believing, as also to the habit by which we believe. When therefore we say that "virtue is the limit of power," virtue is taken for the object of virtue. For the furthest point to which a power can reach, is said to be its virtue; for instance, if a man can carry a hundredweight and not more, his virtue [*In English we should say 'strength,' which is the original signification of the Latin 'virtus': thus we speak of an engine being so many horse-power, to indicate its 'strength'] is put at a hundredweight, and not at sixty. But the objection takes virtue as being essentially the limit of power.

Reply to Objection 2: Good use of free-will is said to be a virtue, in the same sense as above (ad 1); that is to say, because it is that to which virtue is directed as to its proper act. For the act of virtue is nothing else than the good use of free-will.

Reply to Objection 3: We are said to merit by something in two ways. First, as by merit itself, just as we are said to run by running; and thus we merit by acts. Secondly, we are said to merit by something as by the principle whereby we merit, as we are said to run by the motive power; and thus are we said to merit by virtues and habits.

Reply to Objection 4: When we say that virtue is the order or ordering of love, we refer to the end to which virtue is ordered: because in us love is set in order by virtue.

Reply to Objection 5: Natural powers are of themselves determinate to one act: not so the rational powers. And so there is no comparison, as we have said.

Whether human virtue is an operative habit?

Objection 1: It would seem that it is not essential to human virtue to be an operative habit. For Tully says that as health and beauty belong to the body, so virtue belongs to the soul. But health and beauty are not operative habits. Therefore neither is virtue.

Objection 2: Further, in natural things we find virtue not only in reference to act, but also in reference to being: as is clear from the Philosopher, since some have a virtue to be always, while some have a virtue to be not always, but at some definite time. Now as natural virtue is in natural things, so is human virtue in rational beings. Therefore also human virtue is referred not only to act, but also to being.

Objection 3: Further, the Philosopher says (Phys. vii, text. 17) that virtue "is the disposition of a perfect thing to that which is best." Now the best thing to which man needs to be disposed by virtue is God Himself, as Augustine proves (De Moribus Eccl. 3,6, 14) to Whom the soul is disposed by being made like to Him. Therefore it seems that virtue is a quality of the soul in reference to God, likening it, as it were, to Him; and not in reference to operation. It is not, therefore, an operative habit.

On the Contrary: The Philosopher (Ethic. ii, 6) says that "virtue of a thing is that which makes its work good."

I Answer That: Virtue, from the very nature of the word, implies some perfection of power, as we have said above (A[1]). Wherefore, since power [*The one Latin word 'potentia' is rendered 'potentiality' in the first case, and 'power' in the second] is of two kinds, namely, power in reference to being, and power in reference to act; the perfection of each of these is called virtue. But power in reference to being is on the part of matter, which is potential being, whereas power in reference to act, is on the part of the form, which is the principle of action, since everything acts in so far as it is in act.

Now man is so constituted that the body holds the place of matter, the soul that of form. The body, indeed, man has in common with other animals;

and the same is to be said of the forces which are common to the soul and body: and only those forces which are proper to the soul, namely, the rational forces, belong to man alone. And therefore, human virtue, of which we are speaking now, cannot belong to the body, but belongs only to that which is proper to the soul. Wherefore human virtue does not imply reference to being, but rather to act. Consequently it is essential to human virtue to be an operative habit.

Reply to Objection 1: Mode of action follows on the disposition of the agent: for such as a thing is, such is its act. And therefore, since virtue is the principle of some kind of operation, there must needs pre-exist in the operator in respect of virtue some corresponding disposition. Now virtue causes an ordered operation. Therefore virtue itself is an ordered disposition of the soul, in so far as, to wit, the powers of the soul are in some way ordered to one another, and to that which is outside. Hence virtue, inasmuch as it is a suitable disposition of the soul, is like health and beauty, which are suitable dispositions of the body. But this does not hinder virtue from being a principle of operation.

Reply to Objection 2: Virtue which is referred to being is not proper to man; but only that virtue which is referred to works of reason, which are proper to man.

Reply to Objection 3: As God's substance is His act, the highest likeness of man to God is in respect of some operation. Wherefore, as we have said above (Q[3], A[2]), happiness or bliss by which man is made most perfectly conformed to God, and which is the end of human life, consists in an operation.

Whether human virtue is a good habit?

Objection 1: It would seem that it is not essential to virtue that it should be a good habit. For sin is always taken in a bad sense. But there is a virtue even of sin; according to 1 Cor. 15:56: "The virtue of sin is the Law." Therefore virtue is not always a good habit.

Objection 2: Further, Virtue corresponds to power. But power is not only referred to good, but also to evil: according to Is. 5: "Woe to you that are mighty to drink wine, and stout men at drunkenness." Therefore virtue also is referred to good and evil.

Objection 3: Further, according to the Apostle (2 Cor. 12:9): "Virtue is made perfect in infirmity." But infirmity is an evil. Therefore virtue is referred not only to good, but also to evil.

On the Contrary: Augustine says (De Moribus Eccl. vi): "No one can doubt that virtue makes the soul exceeding good": and the Philosopher says (Ethic. ii, 6): "Virtue is that which makes its possessor good, and his work good likewise."

I Answer That: As we have said above (A[1]), virtue implies a perfection of power: wherefore the virtue of a thing is fixed by the limit of its power (De Coelo i). Now the limit of any power must needs be good: for all evil implies defect; wherefore Dionysius says (Div. Hom. ii) that every evil is a weakness. And for this reason the virtue of a thing must be regarded in reference to good. Therefore human virtue which is an operative habit, is a good habit, productive of good works.

Reply to Objection 1: Just as bad things are said metaphorically to be perfect, so are they said to be good: for we speak of a perfect thief or robber; and of a good thief or robber, as the Philosopher explains (Metaph. v, text. 21). In this way therefore virtue is applied to evil things: so that the "virtue" of sin is said to be law, in so far as occasionally sin is aggravated through the law, so as to attain to the limit of its possibility.

Reply to Objection 2: The evil of drunkenness and excessive drink, consists in a falling away from the order of reason. Now it happens that, together with this falling away from reason, some lower power is perfect in reference to that which belongs to its own kind, even in direct opposition to reason, or with some falling away therefrom. But the perfection of that power, since it is compatible with a falling away from reason, cannot be called a human virtue.

Reply to Objection 3: Reason is shown to be so much the more perfect, according as it is able to overcome or endure more easily the weakness of the body and of the lower powers. And therefore human virtue, which is attributed to reason, is said to be "made perfect in infirmity," not of the reason indeed, but of the body and of the lower powers.

Whether virtue is suitably defined?

Objection 1: It would seem that the definition, usually given, of virtue, is not suitable, to wit: "Virtue is a good quality of the mind, by which we live righteously, of which no one can make bad use, which God works in us, without us." For virtue is man's goodness, since virtue it is that makes its subject good. But goodness does not seem to be good, as neither is whiteness white. It is therefore unsuitable to describe virtue as a "good quality."

Objection 2: Further, no difference is more common than its genus; since it is that which divides the genus. But good is more common than quality, since it is convertible with being. Therefore "good" should not be put in the definition of virtue, as a difference of quality.

Objection 3: Further, as Augustine says (De Trin. xii, 3): "When we come across anything that is not common to us and the beasts of the field, it is something appertaining to the mind." But there are virtues even of the irrational parts; as the Philosopher says (Ethic. iii, 10). Every virtue, therefore, is not a good quality "of the mind."

Objection 4: Further, righteousness seems to belong to justice; whence the righteous are called just. But justice is a species of virtue. It is therefore unsuitable to put "righteous" in the definition of virtue, when we say that virtue is that "by which we live righteously."

Objection 5: Further, whoever is proud of a thing, makes bad use of it. But many are proud of virtue, for Augustine says in his Rule that "pride lies in wait for good works in order to slay them." It is untrue, therefore, "that no one can make bad use of virtue."

Objection 6: Further, man is justified by virtue. But Augustine commenting on John 15:11: "He shall do greater things than these," says [*Tract. xxvii in Joan.: Serm. xv de Vcrb. Ap. 11]: "He who created thee without thee, will not justify thee without thee." It is therefore unsuitable to say that "God works virtue in us, without us."

On the Contrary: We have the authority of Augustine from whose words this definition is gathered, and principally in De Libero Arbitrio ii, 19.

I Answer That: This definition comprises perfectly the whole essential notion of virtue. For the perfect essential notion of anything is gathered from all its causes. Now the above definition comprises all the causes of virtue. For the formal cause of virtue, as of everything, is gathered from its genus and difference, when it is defined as "a good quality": for "quality" is the genus of virtue, and the difference, "good." But the definition would be more suitable if for "quality" we substitute "habit," which is the proximate genus. Now virtue has no matter "out of which" it is formed, as neither has any other accident; but it has matter "about which" it is concerned, and matter "in which" it exits, namely, the subject. The matter about which virtue is concerned is its object, and this could not be included in the above definition, because the object fixes the virtue to a certain species, and here we are giving the definition of virtue in general. And so for material cause we have the subject, which is mentioned when we say that virtue is a good quality "of the mind."

The end of virtue, since it is an operative habit, is operation. But it must be observed that some operative habits are always referred to evil, as vicious habits: others are sometimes referred to good, sometimes to evil; for instance, opinion is referred both to the true and to the untrue: whereas virtue is a habit which is always referred to good: and so the distinction of virtue from those habits which are always referred to evil, is expressed in the words "by which we live righteously": and its distinction from those habits which are sometimes directed unto good, sometimes unto evil, in the words, "of which no one makes bad use."

Lastly, God is the efficient cause of infused virtue, to which this definition applies; and this is expressed in the words "which God works in us without us." If we omit this phrase, the remainder of the definition will apply to all virtues in general, whether acquired or infused.

Reply to Objection 1: That which is first seized by the intellect is being: wherefore everything that we apprehend we consider as being, and consequently as gone, and as good, which are convertible with being. Wherefore we say that essence is being and is one and is good; and that oneness is being and one and good: and in like manner goodness. But this is not the case with specific forms, as whiteness and health; for everything that we apprehend, is not apprehended with the notion of white and healthy. We must, however, observe that, as accidents and non-subsistent forms are called beings, not as if they themselves had being, but because things are by them; so also are they called good or one, not by some distinct goodness or oneness, but because by them something is good or one. So also is virtue called "good" because by it something is good.

Reply to Objection 2: Good, which is put in the definition of virtue, is not good in general which is convertible with being, and which extends further than quality, but the good as fixed by reason, with regard to which Dionysius says (Div. Nom. iv) "that the good of the soul is to be in accord with reason."

Reply to Objection 3: Virtue cannot be in the irrational part of the soul, except in so far as this participates in the reason (Ethic. i, 13). And therefore reason, or the mind, is the proper subject of virtue.

Reply to Objection 4: Justice has a righteousness of its own by which it puts those outward things right which come into human use, and are the proper matter of justice, as we shall show further. But the righteousness which denotes order to a due end and to the Divine law, which is the rule of the human will, as stated above (Q[19], A[4]), is common to all virtues.

Reply to Objection 5: One can make bad use of a virtue objectively, for instance by having evil thoughts about a virtue, e.g. by hating it, or by being proud of it: but one cannot make bad use of virtue as principle of action, so that an act of virtue be evil.

Reply to Objection 6: Infused virtue is caused in us by God without any action on our part, but not without our consent. This is the sense of the words, "which God works in us without us."

As to those things which are done by us, God causes them in us, yet not without action on our part, for He works in every will and in every nature.
x

THE METAPHYSICS OF MORALS
by Immanuel Kant

I

Nothing can possibly be conceived in the world, or even out of it, which can be called good, without qualification, except for a good will. Intelligence, wit, judgment, and the other talents of the mind, however they may be named, or courage, resolution, perseverance, as qualities of temperament, are undoubtedly good and desirable in many respects; but these gifts of nature may also become extremely bad and mischievous if the will which is to make use of them, and which, therefore, constitutes what is called character, is not good. It is the same with the gifts of fortune. Power, riches, honor, even health, and the general well-being and contentment with one's life which is called happiness, inspire pride, and often presumption, if there is not a good will to correct the influence of these on the mind, and with this also to rectify the whole principle of acting and adapt it to its end. The sight of a being who is not adorned with a single feature of a pure and good will, enjoying unbroken prosperity, can never give pleasure to an impartial rational spectator. Thus a good will appears to constitute the indispensable condition even of a being worthy of happiness.

There are some qualities which are of service to this good will itself and may facilitate its action, yet which have no intrinsic unconditional value, but always presuppose a good will, and this qualifies the esteem that we justly have for them and does not permit us to regard them as absolutely good. Moderation in the affections and passions, self-control, and calm deliberation are not only good in many respects, but even seem to constitute part of the intrinsic worth of a human being; but they are far from deserving to be called good without qualification, although they have been so unconditionally praised by the ancients. For without the principle of a good will, they may become extremely bad, and the coolness of a villain not only makes him far more dangerous, but also directly makes him more diabolical in our eyes than he would have been without it.

A good will is good not because of what it performs or effects, not by its aptness to attainment of some proposed end, but simply by virtue of the volition; that is, it is good in itself, and considered by itself is to be esteemed much higher than all that can be brought about by it in favor of any inclination, even of the sum total of all inclinations. Even if it should happen that, owing to special disfavor of fortune, or the miserly provision of a step-motherly nature, this will should wholly lack power to accomplish its purpose, if with its greatest efforts it should achieve nothing, and there should remain only the good will (not, to be sure, a mere wish, but the summoning of all means in our power), then, like a jewel, it would still shine by its own light, as a thing which has its whole value in itself. Its usefulness or fruitlessness can neither add nor take away anything from its value. It would be, as it were, only the setting to enable us to handle it the more conveniently in common commerce, or to attract to it the attention of those who are not yet experts, but not to recommend it to true experts, or to determine its value.

There is, however, something so strange in this idea of the absolute value of the mere will, in which no account is taken of its usefulness, that notwithstanding the thorough assent of even common reason to the idea, a suspicion must arise that it may perhaps really be the product of a mere high-flown fancy, and that we may have misunderstood the purpose of nature in assigning reason as the governor of our will. Therefore we will examine this idea from this point of view.

In the physical constitution of an organized being, that is, a being adapted suitably to the purposes of life, we assume it as a fundamental principle that no organ for any purpose will be found but that which is the most fit and best adapted for its purpose. Now in a being which has reason and a will, if the proper object of nature were its conservation, its welfare, in a word, its happiness, then nature would have hit upon a very bad arrangement in selecting the reason of the creature to carry out this purpose. For all the actions which the creature has to perform with a view to this purpose, and the whole rule of its conduct, would be far more surely guided by instinct, and the end of happiness would be attained much more certainly than it ever could be by reason. Should reason have been given to this favored creature over and above, it must only have been to contemplate the happy constitution of its nature, to admire it, to congratulate itself for it, and to feel thankful for it to the beneficial cause, but not that it should subject its desires to that weak and delusive guidance and meddle ineptly with the purpose of nature. In a word, nature would have taken care that reason should not break forth into practical exercise, nor have the presumption, with its weak insight, to think out for itself the plan of happiness, and of the means of attaining it. Nature would not only have taken on herself the choice of the ends, but also of the means, and would have been much more wise to have entrusted both to instinct.

And, in fact, we find that the more cultivated reason applies itself with deliberate purpose to the enjoyment of life and happiness, so much more does the man not reach true satisfaction. And from this circumstance there arises in many, if they are candid enough to confess it, a certain degree of misology, that is, a hatred of reason, especially in the case of those who are most experienced in the use of it, because after calculating all the advantages they derive, I do not say from the invention of all the arts of common luxury, but even from the sciences (which seem to them to be after all only a luxury of the understanding), they find that they have, in fact, only brought more trouble on their shoulders, rather than gaining in happiness; and they end by envying, rather than despising, the more common stamp of men who keep to the guidance of mere instinct and do not allow their reason much influence on their conduct. And this we must admit, that the judgment of those who would much lower the lofty eulogies of the advantages which reason gives us in regard to the happiness and satisfaction of life, or who would even reduce them below zero, is by no means ungrateful to the goodness with which the world is governed, but that there lies at the root of these judgments the idea that our existence has a different and far nobler end, for which reason is properly intended, and which must, therefore, be regarded as the supreme condition to which the private ends of man must, for the most part, be deferred to.

For as reason is not competent to guide the will with certainty in regard to its objects and the satisfaction of all our wants, this being an end to which instinct would have led with much greater certainty; and since, nevertheless, reason is imparted to us as a practical faculty, i.e., as one which is to have influence on the will, therefore, admitting that nature generally in the distribution of her capacities has adapted the means to the end, its true destination must be to produce a will, not merely good as a means to something else, but good in itself, for which reason was absolutely necessary. This will then, though not indeed the sole and complete good, must be the supreme good and the condition of every other, even of the desire of happiness. Under these circumstances, there is nothing inconsistent with the wisdom of nature in the fact that the cultivation of reason, which is required for the first and unconditional purpose, does in many ways interfere, at least in this life, with the attainment of the second, which is always conditional, namely, happiness. It may even reduce it to nothing, without nature failing its purpose. For reason recognizes the establishment of a good will as its highest practical goal, and in attaining this is capable only of a satisfaction of its own proper kind.

We have then to develop the notion of a will which deserves to be highly esteemed for itself and is good without a view to anything further, a notion which exists already in the sound natural understanding, requiring rather to be cleared up than to be taught, and which in estimating the value of our actions always takes the first place and constitutes the condition of all the rest. In order to do this, we will take the notion of duty, which includes that of a good will, although implies certain subjective restrictions and hindrances. These, however, far from concealing it, or rendering it unrecognizable, rather bring it out into the light and make it shine forth so much more the brighter.

I omit here all actions that are already recognized as being inconsistent with duty, although they may be useful for this or that purpose, for with these the question whether they are done from duty cannot arise at all, since they even conflict with it. I also set aside those actions that already conform to duty, but of which men have no direct inclination, performing them because they are compelled by some other inclination. For in this case we can readily distinguish whether the action that agrees with duty is done from duty, or from selfishness. It is much harder to make this distinction when the action accords with duty and the subject has a direct inclination to it. For example, it is always a matter of duty that a merchant should not overcharge an inexperienced customer; and wherever there is much commerce the prudent tradesman does not overcharge, but keeps a fixed price for everyone, so that a child buys of him as well as any other. Men are thus honestly served; but this is not enough to make us believe that the tradesman has acted from duty and from principles of honesty: his own advantage required it; it is out of the question in this case to suppose that he might besides have a direct inclination in favor of the buyers, so that, as it were, from love he should give no advantage to one over another. Thus the action was done neither from duty nor from direct inclination, but merely with a selfish view.

On the other hand, it is a duty to preserve one's life; and everyone has a direct inclination to do so. But on this account the anxious care which most men take for their lives has no intrinsic worth, and their maxim has no moral import. They preserve their life as duty requires but not because duty requires. On the other hand, if adversity and hopeless sorrow have completely taken away the will to live; if that man, strong in mind, indignant at his fate rather than despondent or dejected, wishes for death, and yet preserves his life without loving it—not from inclination or fear, but from duty— then his maxim has moral worth.

To be a philanthropist when we can is a duty; and besides this, there are many minds so sympathetically constituted that, without any other motive of pride or self-interest, they find pleasure in spreading joy around them and take delight in helping others in so far as it is their own work. But I maintain that in such a case an action of this kind, however proper, however amiable it may be, has nevertheless no true moral worth, but is on a level with other inclinations, e.g., the inclination to honor, which, if it is happily directed to that which is in accord with duty and consequently honorable, deserves praise and encouragement, but not esteem. For the maxim lacks the moral import, namely, that such actions be done from duty, not from inclination. Put to the case that the mind of that philanthropist was clouded by sorrow of his own, extinguishing all sympathy to others, and that, while he still has the power to benefit others in distress, he is not touched by their trouble because he is absorbed in his own; and now suppose that he tears himself out of this dead insensibility, and performs the action without any inclination to it, but simply from duty, then his action has genuine moral worth. Further still; if nature has put little sympathy in the heart of this man; if he, supposed to be an upright man, is by temperament cold and indifferent to the sufferings of others, perhaps because in respect of his own he is provided with the special gift of patience and fortitude and supposes, or even requires, that others should have the same—and such a man would certainly not be the meanest product of nature—but if nature had not specially framed him to be a philanthropist, would he not still find in himself a source from which to give himself a far higher worth than that of a good-natured temperament could? Unquestionably. It is in this that the moral worth of the character is brought out which is incomparably the highest of all, namely, that he is a philanthropist, not from inclination, but from duty...

Thus the moral worth of an action does not lie in the result expected from it, nor in any principle of action which requires it to borrow its motive from this result. For all of these results—regardless of one's condition and even the promotion of the happiness of others—could have been brought about by other causes, so that there would have been no need of the will of a rational being; it is in this alone that the supreme good can be found. The preeminent good which we call moral can therefore consist in nothing else than the concept of duty in itself, which is only possible in a rational being, in so far as this concept, and not the result expected from it, determines the will. This is a good already present in the person who acts accordingly, and we do not have to wait for it to appear first in the result...

II

Everything in nature works according to laws. Rational beings alone have the faculty of acting according to the concept of laws, that is according to principles, i.e., have a will. Since the deduction of actions from principles requires reason, the will is nothing but practical reason. If reason infallibly determines the will, then the actions of such a being that are recognized as objectively necessary are subjectively necessary also, i.e., the will is a faculty to choose that only which reason independent of inclination recognizes as practically necessary, i.e., as good. But if reason itself does not sufficiently determine the will, if the latter is influenced also by subjective conditions (particular impulses) which do not always coincide with the objective conditions of a given situation; in a word, if the will does not in itself completely accord with reason (which is actually the case with all men), then the actions which objectively are recognized as necessary are subjectively contingent, and the determination of such a will according to objective laws is obligation, that is to say, the relation of the objective laws to a will that is not thoroughly good is conceived as the determination of the will of a rational being by principles of reason, but of which the will by its nature does not necessarily follow.

Now all imperatives command either hypothetically or categorically. The former represent the practical necessity of a possible action as means to something else that is willed (or at least one that might possibly be willed). The categorical imperative is that which represented an action as necessary in itself without reference to any other end; as objectively necessary.

Since every practical law represents a possible action as good and, on this account, for a subject who is practically determinable by reason, necessary, all imperatives are a formula determining an action which is necessary according to the principle of a will good in some respects. If now the action is good only as a means to something else, then the imperative is hypothetical; if then it is conceived as good in itself and consequently as being necessarily the principle of a will which itself conforms to reason, then it is categorical...

There is, however, one end that can be presupposed as actual in the case of all rational beings, and therefore one purpose that they not merely could have but that we can safely presuppose they all actually do have by a natural necessity, and that purpose is happiness.

Now skill in the choice of means to his own greatest well-being may be called prudence, in the narrowest sense. And thus the imperative that refers to the choice of means to one's own happiness, i.e., the precept of prudence, is still always hypothetical; for the action is not commanded absolutely, but only as means to another purpose.

The word prudence is taken in two senses: in one it may mean knowledge of the world, in the other it may mean knowledge of oneself. The former is a man's ability to influence others so as to use them for his own purposes. The latter is the wisdom to combine all of these purposes for his own lasting benefit. The latter is that to which the value even of the former is reduced, and when a man is prudent in the former sense, but not in the latter, we might better say of him that he is clever and cunning, but, on the whole, still imprudent.

Finally, there is an imperative which commands a certain conduct immediately, without having as its condition any other purpose to be attained by it. This imperative is categorical. It concerns not the matter of the action, or its intended result, but its form and the principle of which it is itself a result; and what is essentially good in it consists in the mental disposition, no matter what the consequences. This imperative may be called that of morality...

When I conceive of a hypothetical imperative, in general I do not know beforehand what it will contain until I am given the condition. But when I conceive of a categorical imperative, I know at once what it contains. For the imperative contains besides the law only the necessity that the maxims shall conform to this law, while the law contains no conditions restricting it, there remains nothing but the general statement that the maxim of the action should conform to a universal law, and it is this conformity alone that the imperative properly represents as necessary.

There is therefore but one categorical imperative namely, this: Act only on that maxim through which one can at the same time will that it should become a universal law...

We now enumerate a few duties, adopting the usual division of them into duties to ourselves and duties to others, and into perfect and imperfect duties.

1. A man reduced to despair by a series of misfortunes feels wearied by life, but is still so far in possession of his reason that he can ask himself whether it would not be contrary to his duty to himself to take his own life. Now he inquires whether the maxim of his action could become a universal law of nature. His maxim is:

> From self-love I adopt it as a principle to shorten my life when its longer duration is likely to bring more pain than satisfaction.

That man then simply asks whether this principle founded on self-love can become a universal law of nature. Now we see at once that a system of nature by which it would be a law to destroy life by means of the very same feeling of self-love whose special nature it is to move man towards the improvement of life would contradict itself and, therefore, could not exist as a system of nature; hence that maxim cannot possibly exist as a universal law of nature and, consequently, would be wholly inconsistent with the principle duty.

2. Another finds himself forced by necessity to borrow money. He knows that he will not be able to repay it, but sees also that nothing will be lent to

him unless he promises to repay it and repay it in a definite time. He desires to make this promise, but he still has the conscience as to ask himself:

> *Is it not unlawful and inconsistent with duty to get out of a difficulty in this way?*

Suppose however that he resolves to do so: then the maxim of his action would be expressed as:

> *When I think myself in want of money, I will borrow money and promise to repay it, although I know I never can do so.*

Now this principle of self-love or of one's own advantage may perhaps be consistent with my whole future welfare; but the question now is, "Is it right?" I change then the suggestion of self-love into a universal law, and state the question as:

> *"How would it be if my maxim were a universal law?"*

Then I see at once that it could never hold as a universal law of nature, but would necessarily contradict itself. For suppose it to be a universal law that everyone when he thinks himself in difficulty should be able to promise whatever he pleases, with the intention of not keeping his promise, the promise itself would become impossible, as well as the end that one might have in view in it, since no one would consider that anything was earnestly promised to him, but would ridicule all such false promises as vain pretenses.

3.   A third finds in himself gifted with a talent that, with the help of some education and culture, might make him a useful man in many respects. But he finds himself in comfortable circumstances and prefers to indulge in pleasure rather than to take pains in enlarging and improving his natural gifts. He asks, however, whether his maxim of neglect of his natural gifts, besides agreeing with his inclination to indulgence, agrees also with what is called duty. He sees then that a system of nature could indeed subsist with such a universal law although men should let their talents waste away and resolve to devote their lives merely to idleness, amusement, and the propagation of their own species- in a word, to enjoyment; but he cannot possibly will that this should become a universal law of nature, or be implanted in us as such by a natural instinct. For, as a rational being, he necessarily knows that his gifts should be developed, since they serve him and have been given to him for all sorts of possible purposes.

4.   A fourth, who is materially wealthy, sees that others have to contend with great poverty and that he could possibly help them, thinks:

> *What concern is it of mine? Let everyone be as happy as Heaven pleases, or as he can make himself; I will take nothing from him nor even envy him, only I do not wish to contribute anything to his welfare or to assist him in his distress!*

Now no doubt if such a mode of thinking were a universal law, the human race might very well subsist and doubtless even better than in a state in which everyone talks of sympathy and good-will, and even occasionally puts them into practice, but, on the other hand, also cheats when he can, betrays the rights of men, or otherwise violates them. Although it is possible that a law of nature might exist in accord with this maxim, it is impossible to will that such a principle should have the validity of a law of nature. For a will that holds this would contradict itself, inasmuch as many cases might occur in which one would have need of the help and sympathy of others, and in which, by such a law sprung from his own will, he would deprive himself of all hope of the help and sympathy of others.

These are a few of the many actual duties, or at least what we regard as such, which obviously fall into two classes on the one principle that we have laid down. We must be able to will that a maxim of our action should become a universal law.[xi]

UTILITARIANISM
by J. S. Mill

The creed which accepts as the foundation of morals, utility, or the greatest happiness principle, holds that actions are right in proportion as they tend to promote happiness, wrong as they tend to produce the reverse of happiness. By happiness is intended pleasure, and the absence of pain; by unhappiness, pain, and the privation of pleasure. To give a clear view of the moral standard set up by the theory, much more requires to be said; in particular, what things it includes in the ideas of pain and pleasure; and to what extent this is left an open question. But these supplementary explanations do not affect the theory of life on which this theory of morality is grounded--namely, that pleasure, and freedom from pain, are the only things desirable as ends; and that all desirable things (which are as numerous in the utilitarian as in any other scheme) are desirable either for the pleasure inherent in themselves, or as means to the promotion of pleasure and the prevention of pain.

Now, such a theory of life excites in many minds, and among them in some of the most estimable in feeling and purpose, inveterate dislike. To suppose that life has (as they express it) no higher end than pleasure—no better and nobler object of desire and pursuit—they designate as utterly mean and groveling; as a doctrine worthy only of swine, to whom the followers of Epicurus were, at a very early period, contemptuously likened; and modern holders of the doctrine are occasionally made the subject of equally polite comparisons by its German, French, and English assailants.

When thus attacked, the Epicureans have always answered, that it is not they, but their accusers, who represent human nature in a degrading light; since the accusation supposes human beings to be capable of no greater pleasures except those of which swine are capable. If this supposition were true, the charge could not be denied, but would then be no longer attributed; for if the sources of pleasure were precisely the same to human beings and to swine, the rule of life which is good enough for the one would be good enough for the other. The comparison of the Epicurean life to that of beasts is felt to be degrading, precisely because a beast's pleasures do not satisfy a human being's conceptions of happiness. Human beings have faculties more elevated than the animal appetites, and when once made conscious of them, do not regard anything as happiness which does not include their gratification. I do not, indeed, consider the Epicureans to have been by any means faultless in drawing out their scheme of consequences from the utilitarian principle. To do this in any sufficient manner, many Stoic, as well as Christian elements require to be included. But there is no known Epicurean theory of life which does not assign to the pleasures of the intellect; of the feelings and imagination, and of the moral sentiments, a much higher value as pleasures than to those of mere sensation. It must be admitted, however, that utilitarian writers in general have placed the superiority of mental over bodily pleasures chiefly in the greater duration, safety, and lack of cost of the former--that is, in their circumstantial advantages rather than in their intrinsic nature. And on all these points utilitarians have fully proved their case; but they might have taken the other, and, as it may be called, higher ground, with entire consistency. It is quite compatible with the principle of utility to recognize the fact, that some kinds of pleasure are more desirable and more valuable than others. It would be absurd that while, in estimating all other things, quality is considered as well as quantity, the estimation of pleasures should be supposed to depend on quantity alone.

If I am asked, what I mean by difference of quality in pleasures, or what makes one pleasure more valuable than another, merely as a pleasure, except its being greater in amount, there is but one possible answer. Of two pleasures, if there be one to which all or almost all who have experience of both give a decided preference, irrespective of any feeling of moral obligation to prefer it, that is the more desirable pleasure. If one of the two is, by those who are competently acquainted with both, placed so far above the other that they prefer it, even though knowing it to involve a greater effort, and would not quit from it for any quantity of the other pleasure which their nature is capable of, we are justified in ascribing to the preferred enjoyment a superiority in quality, so far outweighing quantity as to render it, in comparison, of small account.

Now it is an unquestionable fact that those who are equally acquainted with, and equally capable of appreciating and enjoying, both, do give a most marked preference to the manner of existence which employs their higher faculties. Few human creatures would consent to be changed into any one of the lower animals, for a promise of the fullest allowance of a beast's pleasures; no intelligent human being would consent to be a fool, no instructed person would be ignorant, no person of feeling and conscience would be selfish and base, even though they should be persuaded that the fool, the ignorant, or the rascal is better satisfied with his lot than they are with theirs. They would not resign what they possess more than he, for the most complete satisfaction of all the desires which they have in common with him. If they ever fancy they would, it is only in cases of unhappiness so extreme, that to escape from it they would exchange their lot for almost any other, however undesirable in their own eyes.

A being of higher faculties requires more to make him happy, is capable probably of more acute suffering, and is certainly accessible to it at more points, than one of an inferior type; but in spite of these liabilities, he can never really wish to sink into what he feels to be a lower grade of existence. We may give what explanation we please of this unwillingness; we may attribute it to pride, a name which is given indiscriminately to some of the most and to some of the least estimable feelings of which mankind are capable; we may refer it to the love of liberty and personal independence, an appeal to which was with the Stoics one of the most effective means for the inculcation of it; to the love of power, or to the love of excitement, both of which do really enter into and contribute to it: but its most appropriate name is a sense of dignity, which all human beings possess in one form or other, and in some, though by no means in exact, proportion to their higher faculties, and which is so essential a part of the happiness of those in whom it is strong, that nothing which conflicts with it could be, otherwise than momentarily, an object of desire to them.

Whoever supposes that this preference takes place at a sacrifice of happiness—that the superior being, in anything like equal circumstances, is not happier than the inferior—confounds the two very different ideas, of happiness, and content. It is indisputable that the being whose capacities of enjoyment are low, has the greatest chance of having them fully satisfied; and a highly-endowed being will always feel that any happiness which he can look for, as the world is constituted, is imperfect. But he can learn to bear its imperfections, if they are at all bearable; and they will not make him envy the being who is indeed unconscious of the imperfections, but only because he feels not at all the good which those imperfections qualify. It is better to be a human being dissatisfied than a pig satisfied; better to be Socrates dissatisfied than a fool satisfied. And if the fool, or the pig, is of a different opinion, it is because they only know their own side of the question. While the other party to the comparison knows both sides.

It may be objected, that many who are capable of the higher pleasures, occasionally, under the influence of temptation, postpone them to the lower. But this is quite compatible with a full appreciation of the intrinsic superiority of the higher. Men often, from infirmity of character, make their election for the nearer good, though they know it to be the less valuable; and this no less when the choice is between two bodily pleasures, than when it is between bodily and mental. They pursue sensual indulgences to the injury of health, though perfectly aware that health is the greater good. It may be further objected, that many who begin with youthful enthusiasm for everything noble, as they advance in years sink into indolence and selfishness. But I do not believe that those who undergo this very common change, voluntarily choose the lower description of pleasures in preference to the higher. I believe that before they devote themselves exclusively to the one, they have already become incapable of the other.

Capacity for the nobler feelings is in most natures a very tender plant, easily killed, not only by hostile influences, but by mere want of sustenance; and in the majority of young persons it speedily dies away if the occupations to which their position in life has devoted them, and the society into which it has thrown them, are not favorable to the exercise of the higher capacity. Men lose their high aspirations as they lose their intellectual tastes, because they have not time or opportunity for indulging them; and they become addicted to inferior pleasures, not because they deliberately prefer them, but because they are either the only ones to which they have access, or the only ones which they are any longer capable of enjoying. It may be questioned whether anyone who has remained equally susceptible to both classes of pleasures, ever knowingly and calmly preferred the lower; though many, in all ages, have broken down in an ineffectual attempt to combine both.

From this verdict of the only competent judges, I apprehend there can be no appeal. On the question of which is the best worth having of two pleasures the judgment of those who are qualified by knowledge of both, or, if they differ, that of the majority among them, must be admitted as final. And there should be less hesitation in accepting this judgment respectful to the quality of pleasures, since there is no other tribunal to be referred to even on the question of quantity. What means are there of determining which is the more acute of two pains, or the more intense of two pleasurable sensations, except the experience of those who are familiar with both? Neither pains nor pleasures are alike, and pain is always different than pleasure. What is there to decide whether a particular pleasure is worth purchasing at the cost of a particular pain, except the feelings and judgment of the experienced? When, therefore, those feelings and judgments declare the pleasures derived from the higher faculties to be preferable in kind, apart from the question of intensity, to those of the animal nature they are entitled on this subject to the same regard.

I have dwelt on this point, as being a necessary part of a perfectly just conception of utility or happiness, considered as a direct rule of human conduct. But it is by no means an indispensable condition to the acceptance of the utilitarian standard; for that standard is not the agent's own greatest happiness, but the greatest amount of happiness altogether; and if it may possibly be doubted whether a noble character is always the happier for its nobleness, there can be no doubt that it makes other people happier, and that the world in general is immensely made better by it. Utilitarianism, therefore, could only attain its end by the general cultivation of nobleness of character, even if each individual were only benefited by the nobleness of others, and his own, so far as happiness is concerned, were a sheer deduction from the benefit. But the bare pronouncement of such an absurdity as this last, renders refutation unnecessary.

According to the greatest happiness principle, as above explained, the ultimate end, with reference to and for the sake of which all other things are desirable (whether we are considering our own good or that of other people), is an existence exempt as far as possible from pain, and as rich as possible in enjoyments, both in point of quantity and quality; the test of quality, and the rule for measuring it against quantity, being the preference felt by those who, in their opportunities of experience, to which must be added their habits of self-consciousness and self-observation, are best furnished with the means of comparison. This, being, according to the utilitarian opinion, the end of human action, is necessarily also the standard of morality; which may accordingly be defined, the rules and precepts for human conduct, by the observance of which an existence such as has been described might be, to the greatest extent possible, secured to all mankind; and not to them only, but, so far as the nature of things admits, to the whole sentient creation.

Against this doctrine, however, arises another class of objectors, who say that happiness, in any form, cannot be the rational purpose of human life and action; because, in the first place, it is unattainable: and they contemptuously ask, what right has you to be happy? A question which Mr.

Carlyle clenches by the addition, what right, a short time ago, had you even to be? Next, they say, that men can do without happiness; that all noble human beings have felt this, and could not have become noble but by learning the lesson of renunciation; which lesson, thoroughly learnt and submitted to, they affirm to be the beginning and necessary condition of all virtue.

The first of these objections would go to the root of the matter were it well founded; for if no happiness is to be had at all by human beings, the attainment of it cannot be the end of morality, or of any rational conduct. Though, even in that case, something might still be said for the utilitarian theory; since utility includes not solely the pursuit of happiness, but the prevention or mitigation of unhappiness; and if the former aim be imaginary, there will be all the greater scope and more imperative need for the latter, so long at least as mankind thinks fit to live.

When, however, it is thus positively asserted to be impossible that human life should be happy, the assertion, if not something like a verbal quibble, is at least an exaggeration. If by happiness be meant a continuity of highly pleasurable excitement, it is evident enough that this is impossible. A state of exalted pleasure lasts only moments, or in some cases, and with some intermissions, hours or days, and is the occasional brilliant flash of enjoyment, not its permanent and steady flame. Of this the philosophers who have taught that happiness is the end of life were as fully aware as those who taunt them. The happiness which they meant was not a life of rapture, but moments of such, in an existence made up of few and transitory pains, many and various pleasures, with a decided predominance of the active over the passive, and having as the foundation of the whole, not to expect more from life than it is capable of bestowing. A life thus composed, to those who have been fortunate enough to obtain it, has always appeared worthy of the name of happiness. And such an existence is even now the lot of many, during some considerable portion of their lives. The present wretched education, and wretched social arrangements, are the only real hindrance to its being attainable by almost all.

The objectors perhaps may doubt whether human beings, if taught to consider happiness as the end of life, would be satisfied with such a moderate share of it. But great numbers of mankind have been satisfied with much less. The main constituents of a satisfied life appear to be two, either of which by itself is often found sufficient for the purpose: tranquility, and excitement. With much tranquility, many find that they can be content with very little pleasure: with much excitement, many can reconcile themselves to a considerable quantity of pain. There is assuredly no inherent impossibility in enabling even the mass of mankind to unite both; since the two are so far from being incompatible that they are in natural alliance, the prolongation of either being a preparation for, and exciting a wish for, the other. It is only those in whom indolence amounts to a vice, that do not desire excitement after an interval of rest; it is only those in whom the need of excitement is a disease, that feel the tranquility which follows excitement dull and insipid, instead of pleasurable in direct proportion to the excitement which preceded it.

When people who are fortunate in their outward lot do not find in life sufficient enjoyment to make it valuable to them, the cause generally is, caring for nobody but themselves. To those who have neither public nor private affections, the excitements of life are much curtailed, and in any case dwindle in value as the time approaches when all selfish interests must be terminated by death: while those who leave after them objects of personal affection, and especially those who have also cultivated a fellow-feeling with the collective interests of mankind, retain as lively an interest in life on the eve of death as in the vigor of youth and health. Next to selfishness, the principal cause which makes life unsatisfactory, is want of mental cultivation. A cultivated mind—I do not mean that of a philosopher, but any mind to which the fountains of knowledge have been opened, and which has been taught, in any tolerable degree, to exercise its faculties—finds sources of inexhaustible interest in all that surrounds it; in the objects of nature, the achievements of art, the imaginations of poetry, the incidents of history, the ways of mankind past and present, and their prospects in the future. It is possible to become indifferent to all this, and that too without having exhausted a thousandth part of it; but only when one has had from the beginning no moral or human interest in these things, and has sought in them only the gratification of curiosity.

Now there is absolutely no reason in the nature of things why an amount of mental culture sufficient to give an intelligent interest in these objects of contemplation, should not be the inheritance of every one born in a civilized country. As little is there an inherent necessity that any human being should be an egotist, devoid of every feeling or care but those which centre in his own individuality. Something far superior to this is sufficiently common even now, to give ample example of what the human species may be capable of...

Meanwhile, let utilitarians never cease to claim the morality of self-devotion as a possession which belongs by as good a right to them, as either to the Stoic or to the Transcendentalist. The utilitarian morality does recognize in human beings the power of sacrificing their own greatest good for the good of others. It only refuses to admit that the sacrifice is in itself a good. A sacrifice which does not increase, or tend to increase, the sum total of happiness, it considers as wasted. The only self-renunciation which it applauds, is devotion to the happiness, or to some of the means of happiness, of others; either of mankind collectively, or of individuals within the limits imposed by the collective interests of mankind.

I must again repeat, what the assailants of utilitarianism seldom have the justice to acknowledge, that the happiness which forms the utilitarian standard of what is right in conduct, is not the agent's own happiness, but that of all concerned. As between his own happiness and that of others, utilitarianism requires him to be as strictly impartial as a disinterested and benevolent spectator. In the Golden Rule of Jesus of Nazareth, we read the complete spirit of the ethics of utility. To do as one would be done by, and to love one's neighbor as oneself, constitute the ideal perfection of utilitarian morality. As the means of making the nearest approach to this ideal, utility would enjoin, first, that laws and social arrangements should place the happiness, or (as speaking practically it may be called) the interest, of every individual, as nearly as possible in harmony with the interest of the whole; and secondly, that education and opinion, which have so vast a power over human character, should so use that power as to establish in the mind of every individual an indissoluble association between his own happiness and the good of the whole; especially between his own happiness and the practice of such modes of conduct, negative and positive, as regard for the universal happiness prescribes: so that not only he may be unable to conceive the possibility of happiness for himself, consistently with conduct opposed to the general good, but also that a direct impulse to promote the general good may be in every individual one of the habitual motives of action, and the sentiments connected with it may fill a large and prominent place in every human being's existence. If the critics of the utilitarian morality represented it in their own minds in this its true character, I know not what other morality they could confess to be better than it or what they could affirm to be wanting in it.

The objectors to utilitarianism cannot always be charged with representing it in a discreditable light. On the contrary, those among them who entertain anything like a just idea of its disinterested character, sometimes find fault with its standard as being too high for humanity. They say it is exacting too much to require that people should always act from the promotion of the general interests of society. But this is to mistake the very meaning of a standard of morals, and to confound the rule of action with the motive of it. It is the business of ethics to tell us what are our duties, or by what test we may know them; but no system of ethics requires that the sole motive of all we do should be a feeling of duty; on the contrary, ninety-nine percent of all our actions are done from other motives, and done rightly so, if the rule of duty does not condemn them. It is the more unjust to utilitarianism that this particular misapprehension should be made a ground of objection to it, inasmuch as utilitarian moralists have gone beyond almost all others in affirming that the motive has nothing to do with the morality of the action, though much with the worth of the agent.

He who saves a fellow creature from drowning does what is morally right, whether his motive be duty, or the hope of being paid for his trouble: he who betrays the friend that trusts him, is guilty of a crime, even if his object be to serve another friend to whom he is under greater obligations. But to speak only of actions done from the motive of duty, and in direct obedience to principle: is a misapprehension of the utilitarian mode of thought, to conceive of it as implying that people should fix their minds upon so wide a generality as the world, or society at large. The great majority of good actions are intended, not for the benefit of the world, but for that of individuals, of which the good of the world is made up; and the thoughts of the most virtuous man need not on these occasions travel beyond the particular persons concerned, except so far as it is necessary to assure himself that in benefiting them he is not violating the rights— that is, the legitimate and authorized expectations— of anyone else.

The multiplication of happiness is, according to utilitarian ethics, the object of virtue: the occasions on which any person (except one in a thousand) has it in his power to do this on an extended scale, in other words, to be a public benefactor, are but exceptional; and on these occasions alone is he called on to consider public utility; in every other case, private utility, the interest or happiness of some few persons, is all he has to attend to. Those alone the influence of whose actions extends to society in general, need concern themselves habitually about so large an object. In the case of abstinences indeed—of things which people forbear to do, from moral considerations, though the consequences in the particular case might be beneficial—it would be unworthy of an intelligent agent not to be consciously aware that the action is of a class which, if practiced generally, would be generally injurious, and that this is the ground of the obligation to abstain from it. The amount of regard for the public interest implied in this recognition, is no greater than is demanded by every system of morals; for they all enjoin to abstain from whatever is manifestly harmful to society.

The same considerations apply to another criticism of the doctrine of utility, founded on a still grosser misconception of the purpose of a standard of morality, and of the very meaning of the words right and wrong. It is often affirmed that utilitarianism renders men cold and without sympathy; that it chills their moral feelings towards individuals; that it makes them regard only the dry and hard consideration of the consequences of actions, not taking into their moral estimate the qualities from which those actions arise. If the assertion means that they do not allow their judgment respecting the rightness or wrongness of an action to be influenced by their opinion of the qualities of the person who does it, this is a complaint not against utilitarianism, but against having any standard of morality at all; for certainly no known ethical standard decides an action to be good or bad because it is done by a good or a bad man, still less because done by an amiable, a brave, or a benevolent man or the contrary. These considerations are relevant, not to the estimation of actions, but of persons; and there is nothing in the utilitarian theory inconsistent with the fact that there are other things which interest us in persons besides the rightness and wrongness of their actions.

The Stoics, indeed, with the paradoxical misuse of language which was part of their system, and by which they strove to raise themselves above all concern about anything but virtue, were fond of saying that he who has that has everything; that he, and only he, is rich, is beautiful, is a king. But no claim of this description is made for the virtuous man by the utilitarian doctrine. Utilitarians are quite aware that there are other desirable possessions and qualities besides virtue, and are perfectly willing to allow to all of them their full worth. They are also aware that a right action does not necessarily indicate a virtuous character, and that actions which are blamable often proceed from qualities entitled to praise. When this is apparent in any particular case, it modifies their estimation, not certainly of the act, but of the agent. I grant that they are, notwithstanding, of opinion, that in the long run the best proof of a good character is good actions;

and resolutely refuse to consider any mental disposition as good, of which the predominant tendency is to produce bad conduct. This makes them unpopular with many people; but it is an unpopularity which they must share with everyone who regards the distinction between right and wrong in a serious light; and the reproach is not one which a conscientious utilitarian need be anxious to repel.

If no more is meant by the objection than that many utilitarians look on the morality of actions, as measured by the utilitarian standard, with too exclusive a regard, and do not lay sufficient stress upon the other beauties of character which go towards making a human being loveable or admirable, this may be admitted. Utilitarians who have cultivated their moral feelings, but not their sympathies nor their artistic perceptions, do fall into this mistake; and so do all other moralists under the same conditions. What can be said in excuse for other moralists is equally available for them, namely, that if there is to be any error, it is better that it should be on that side. As a matter of fact, we may affirm that among utilitarians as among adherents of other systems, there is every imaginable degree of rigidity and of laxity in the application of their standard: some are even puritanically rigorous, while others are as indulgent as can possibly be desired by a sinner or by sentimentalist. But on the whole, a doctrine which brings prominently forward the interest that mankind have in the repression and prevention of conduct which violates the moral law, is likely to be inferior to no other in turning the sanctions of opinion against such violations. It is true, the question, "What does violate the moral law?" is one on which those who recognize different standards of morality are likely now and then to differ. But differences of opinion on moral questions was not first introduced into the world by utilitarianism, while that doctrine does supply, if not always an easy, at all events a tangible and intelligible mode of deciding such differences.[xii]

It may not be superfluous to notice a few more of the common misapprehensions of utilitarian ethics, even those which are so obvious and gross that it might appear impossible for any person of candor and intelligence to fall into them: since persons, even of considerable mental endowments, often give themselves so little trouble to understand the bearings of any opinion against which they entertain a prejudice, and men are in general so little conscious of this voluntary ignorance as a defect, that the most vulgar misunderstandings of ethical doctrines are continually met with in the deliberate writings of persons of the greatest pretensions both to high principle and to philosophy.

We not uncommonly hear the doctrine of utility spoken against as a godless doctrine. If it be necessary to say anything at all against so mere an assumption, we may say that the question depends upon what idea we have formed of the moral character of the Deity. If it be a true belief that God desires, above all things, the happiness of his creatures, and that this was his purpose in their creation, utility is not only not a godless doctrine, but more profoundly religious than any other.

If it be meant that utilitarianism does not recognize the revealed will of God as the supreme law of morals, I answer, that a utilitarian who believes in the perfect goodness and wisdom of God, necessarily believes that whatever God has thought fit to reveal on the subject of morals, must fulfil the requirements of utility in a supreme degree. But others have been of opinion that the Christian revelation was intended, and is fitted, to inform the hearts and minds of mankind with a spirit which should enable them to find for themselves what is right, and incline them to do it when found, rather than to tell them, except in a very general way, what it is: and that we need a doctrine of ethics, carefully followed out, to interpret to us the will of God.

A CARE APPROACH
by Rita Manning

An ethic of care is a way of understanding one's moral role, of looking at moral issues and coming to an accommodation in moral situations. In this chapter, I will outline my version of care ethics, and provide an overview of some other important care theories.

One Model of Care Ethics

Though humans have always included features of care in their constructive interactions with each other, it emerged only recently as a systematic moral perspective. Nel Noddings' very influential book, Caring: A Feminine Approach to Ethics and Moral Education, was the first contemporary work that described care in some detail as a moral orientation. (Noddings, 1986, 2003) Virginia Held has also been an influential defender for this perspective who has most recently extended this perspective to the global arena. (Held, 2005) There are important differences and similarities in the different descriptions of an ethic of care, but in this first section, I will be defending my own particular conception of an ethic of care. (Manning, 1992) Care involves a basic human capacity to recognize and respond to the needs of others and to moderate our behavior by appeal to the good or harm it might cause to others. Martin Hoffman is a prominent moral psychologist who sees care as growing out of our natural capacity for empathy. (Hoffman, 2000) This capacity is evident even in newborns, who cry when they hear another baby cry. Later in their development, children come to be motivated to help whenever they encounter others in distress. Finally, reflection allows us to build on our basic empathic distress at the suffering of others. We then can generalize beyond our immediate experience of someone's distress and imagine the distress of someone who is distant from us. In both cases, we feel impelled to help. Because there is a natural basis for care, care as a moral perspective can be both a strong motivation for doing the right thing, and can provide a basis for recognizing right actions.

One way to think about moral perspectives is to see them as growing out of ideal ways to respond in a certain context. For example, if one thinks about what is involved in doing one's moral best in the context of a marketplace between relatively independent and self-interested strangers, the value of honesty and trust are central. When one thinks about what is involved in caring for someone who needs our help, the value of concern, competence and trust are central. The care perspective in moral philosophy grew out of looking systematically at what is required to be a responsible member of a flourishing relationship. Sara Ruddick, for example, looked carefully at what is involved in being a good mother to dependent children. (Ruddick, 1989) Many contemporary defenders of an ethic of care, and many historical antecedents such as David Hume and Adam Smith, think that one can generalize beyond relationships with our intimates. Thus once we find out what values motivate a person to be an ideal caring person in an intimate relationship, one can apply those values to situations that involve distant strangers. When one understands what practices best allow us to apply these values in intimate relationships, then one can extend these practices to other situations.

For care ethics, caring is a moral response to a variety of features of situations: harm, past promises, role relationships etc. In the case of need, our obligation to respond in an appropriately caring way arises when we are able to respond to need. Need is mediated by a number of factors including family, culture, economic class, gender and sexuality, disability and illness. As a caring person responds to needs, she recognizes the vast differences in power that exist and shape the recognition and articulation of needs. Harm is another feature of moral situations. Most people understand that being the cause of harming someone else creates an obligation to respond. But causation is a complex idea. We can be part of the causal story even when we don't think of ourselves as the primary cause. Suppose, for example, that you see the person sitting next to you cheating on an exam. If you simply look the other way and later find out that a patient was seriously harmed because the practitioner really did not understand the procedure they should have followed, and that this procedure was the very one they were being tested on when you saw them cheating, you are partly responsible for the harm.

There are two other things that call up an obligation to care that are worth noting here--past promising and role responsibility. When we make a promise, either explicit or implicit, we commit ourselves to a certain course of action. An ethic of care doesn't say that you are always committed to keeping a promise because sometimes doing so can be harmful to all concerned, but it does impose a moral obligation to respond. Similarly, being in a particular role, e.g. healthcare practitioner, comes with a set of general obligations.

There are four central processes in an ethic of care: moral attention, sympathetic understanding, relationship awareness, and harmony and accommodation.

Moral Attention

Moral attention is the attention to the situation in all its complexity. When one is morally attentive, one wishes to become aware of all the details that will allow a sympathetic response to the situation. It is not enough to know that this is a case of a particular kind, say a case about lying or cruelty. In order to understand what our obligations are, we have to know all the details that might make a difference in our understanding and response to the particular situation at hand.

Sympathetic Understanding

When one sympathetically understands the situation, one is open to sympathizing and even identifying with the persons in the situation. One tries to be aware of what the others in the situation would want one to do, what would most likely be in their best interests, and how they would like one to carry out their wishes and interests and meet their needs. Note that it is not at all clear what is in someone's best interest and that what one desires and what is actually in one's best interest are not identical. Balancing these conflicts requires sensitive dialogue and negotiation. I call this sensitive attention to the best interests of others "maternalism." As one adopts this sympathetic attitude one often becomes aware of what others want and need. Finally, as we respond to others, we look to satisfy their needs in ways that will preserve their sense of competence and dignity while at the same time addressing their needs or alleviating their suffering.

Relationship Awareness

There is a special kind of relationship awareness that characterizes caring. First there is the most basic relationship, that of fellow creatures. Then there is the immediate relationship of need and ability to fill the need. Another relationship is created when you are the cause of harm to someone else. One might also be in some role relationship with the other that calls for a particular response, such as doctor-patient. One is aware of all these relationships as he surveys a situation from the perspective of care. But there is another kind of relationship awareness that is involved as well. One can be aware of the network of relationships that connect humans, and care about preserving and nurturing these relationships. As caring persons think about what to do, they try not to undermine these relationships but rather to nurture and extend the relationships that are supportive of human flourishing.

Accommodation and Harmony

Related to the notion of relationship awareness is accommodation. Often times there are many persons involved and how best to respond is not obvious. The desire to nurture networks of care requires that one try to accommodate the needs of all, including oneself. It is not always possible, or wise, to do what everyone thinks they need, but it is important to give everyone concerned a sense of being involved and considered in the process. When we do this, we have a better chance of preserving harmony. Of course not all harmony is worth preserving. The oppressive society may be pretty stable and harmonious, but at the price of those at the bottom. An ethic of care would be opposed to this type of superficial harmony since it is dependent on treating some as though they do not deserve the same care as others.

Care Appeals to Emotion.

The central emotion in care ethics is empathy. Empathy is a complex of emotional responses, conditioned responses and reflective judgments about how one ought to respond. Martin Hoffman describes empathy as both a response to suffering and as a proactive constraint on behavior. As a response to suffering, empathy provides a motive to alleviate suffering. As a constraint on behavior, empathy provides reason to avoid inflicting harm on others and a reason for providing redress to the victims of harm.

Virginia Held contrasts care with principle-based views by describing care as emotionally based while principle based views are cognitively based. I would argue that care is also reflective and empirically based. One cannot be appropriately caring independently of an assessment of the value of care and the specific demands of the particular relationships and situations one finds oneself in. We have a wealth of evidence about the world and about the concerns and interests of humans to guide us in filling out an account of caring obligation.

Care ethics is not a principle-based accounts-- one doesn't discover one's obligations by reflecting on one's commitments to moral principles. Further, having an obligation toward or for someone doesn't imply that there is one unique way of discharging the obligation. From the care perspective, the morally praiseworthy person acts directly on the motive of care and concern for others and not on the motive of respect for moral principle. In fact, both Noddings and Held argue that moral principles are often used to distance oneself from others. Although I agree that they can function this way, I think they can also serve the useful function of providing moral minimums when our ability to understand the situation is in some sense compromised or when we need a general rule to guide behavior in an institutional setting.

Fifth, for care ethics, the right action becomes clear only in the context of focused attention to the immediate situation. Nel Noddings describes engrossment in the other, while Virginia Held describes moral responsiveness as the device by which one comes to understand one's obligations. I describe moral attention and sympathetic understanding as the process whereby one begins to understand one's particular obligations.

An ethic of care assumes a relationship centered social ontology and corresponding self-understanding. Care theorists assume that persons are at least partly defined by the relationships in which they participate. Nona Lyons argues that a social ontology is common to people who find care ethics more persuasive than some other moral theories, while those whose self-identify is more individualistic will gravitate to other moral theories. (Lyons, 1983) What she calls 'separate/objective selves' recognize moral dilemmas as those that involve a conflict between their principles and someone else's desires, needs or demands. As such, they must mediate their interaction with others in terms of ground rules and procedures that can be accepted by all. At the same time, separate/objective selves recognize that interaction with others plays a role in one's satisfaction, so they value community and relationship insofar as these play a role in individual satisfaction. Connected selves, on the other hand, see themselves in terms of others, so relationship is central to self-identity, rather than seen as voluntary and incidental. The problem of interaction is not then conceived of as how to get others to interact with oneself on terms that would be acceptable to all, but how to protect the ties of affection and connection that are central to one's very self-identity.

Care as a Virtue

Held explicitly rejects the view that care is a virtue, while I think this is the most plausible way to understand it. Like other virtues, care is a general disposition to behave in a particular way. One argument for seeing care as a virtue is that if we fail to do so, we will not be able to trust our natural feelings of empathy to lead us to do the right thing. There are two ways that empathy can fail as a guide to moral action. The first is the failure to feel empathy in the presence of suffering or harm. Conscious avoidance of suffering and blaming the victim are very effective ways to avoid feeling empathy. But the failure to empathize is not always a conscious and deliberate action. Sometimes we are simply overwhelmed by the suffering of others and experience paralyzing empathic over-arousal.

The second way that empathy can fail as a moral motive is bias toward the near and dear. Hoffman distinguishes here between two kinds of empathic bias: here and now bias, and familiarity bias. We are more likely to feel empathy for someone with whom we are in direct contact with than with someone who is more distant, regardless of who is more in need of our help. So if Dorothy comes into your office and really needs your help, you are more likely to help her even if you've just been told that another patient, Jacques, is on the phone and also needs your help. Dorothy's distress calls up reactions that are, to a certain extent, simply hard-wired into your brain while Jacques' predicament requires you to imagine how he is feeling.

Familiarity bias has a similar, probably evolutionary, basis: the groups that survived to reproduce were those groups whose members learned to be altruistic towards each other. If we see care as a virtue, we will be able to explain why the caring person should avoid these failures of empathy. Like other virtues, care is a general disposition to behave in a particular way in all similar situations. If care is a virtue, the person who gives in to the above failures of empathy is an insufficiently caring or benevolent person. Further, ideally caring or benevolent persons would recognize these human failings and consciously work to extend their care to distant others.

The Foundation of Obligation

Annette Baier suggests that a care ethics would not need an account of obligation, because the concept of obligation implies coercion while care implies affection as the basic motivation. (Baier, 1995) She argues that we ought to supplant the concept of obligation with the concept of trust, conceiving of morality as based on trusting rather than coercing people. But I think there are two key distinctions that we can draw here. The first is between what we ought to do and what motives we ought to act upon. While care ethics privileges the motive of concern for others over the motive of concern for doing one's duty, it's not clear that this is incompatible with also recognizing obligations. The second is between having an obligation and having a system for enforcing obligation. This is the classic distinction between obligation and blame. I think it is better to be able to trust people to carry out their obligations than to have to resort to coercion, one cannot even understand trust in this sense without assuming that we do in fact have obligations.

Care and Other Moral Perspectives

At this point, I want to make a meta-ethical point. I am not convinced that in some ethically preferred world, however one defines this, everyone would adopt the same moral theory or the same way of dealing with the moral realities of life. I am certainly not convinced that in this world, everyone can do so. Rather, I think that each reasonably adequate moral theory has insight to offer and sheds light on a different aspect of our moral lives. I also think that each of us has a particular history and moral narrative that limits our ability to adopt new moral perspectives, regardless of how we may evaluate one moral theory against another. Finally, I think that when we try to make moral theories guides to action in the rough and tumble world of complex and difficult choices, we ought to take comfort where and when we can.

It is also important to distinguish between an ethic of care and an ethical approach to care giving. One need not subscribe to an ethic of care as a moral perspective to realize that there are special issues that arise for any of us in our various roles as caregivers. I think that an ethic of care will shed light on a range of issues, certainly including the ethics of care giving, but I am not committed to the view that moral theories are necessarily incompatible. They are often complementary. Care and Confucian ethics are similar in some important respects, for example. Ideal Humanness (jen) and propriety (li) play a central role in Confucian ethics. Jen is analogous in some important respects to care, while li, like accommodation, reminds us that the good society must value harmony among its members. (Tao, 2000)

One helpful way to connect moral theories is to notice that they each focus primarily on a different component of our moral experience. An ethic of care reminds us of the importance of human relationships. It places moral value on communities as well as persons and asserts that our actions take place in the context of relationship--our decisions should consider existing relationships and are often carried out via social action. Doing the right thing and living the morally good life must be understood in the context of trust, reciprocity and concern for others.

An ethic of care provides a corrective to some other ways of thinking about caring for patients. Kantian and utilitarian approaches are often seen as the gold standard in discussions of health care, but they are not quite up to every task. Patient autonomy and patient rights have a distinctly Kantian pedigree. We value patient autonomy because we see humans as rational moral agents who ought to be treated as ends in themselves and never merely as means. Patient rights provide the framework for our interactions with these autonomous persons. But if we rely exclusively on this perspective, we may lose sight of patients as needing care. When we are sick we may not be up to the task of asserting our rights, and while we may value our autonomy we also value being cared for. Utilitarianism is most useful at the macro-level in discussions of social issues, reminding us of problems of cost and allocation. Care reminds us never to lose sight of actual persons. [xiii]

BIBLIOGRAPY

Taken from, <u>The Transposition of Edith Stein: Her Contributions to Philosophy, Feminism, and The Theology of the Body</u>. By John C. Wilhelmsson. San Jose: Chaos To Order Publishing, 2012. Used by permission.

[ii] This translation of Plato's Republic originally by Benjamin Jowett in 1894 with revisions by the editor.

[iii] This translation of Aristotle's Ethics originally by D. P. Chase in 1915 with revisions by the editor.

[iv] Taken from, <u>Ancient and Modern Celebrated Freethinkers.</u> Reprinted from <u>Half-Hours With The Freethinkers</u>. by "Iconoclast.", A. Collins, and J. Watts ("Iconoclast", pseud. of Charles Bradlaugh). Edited by "Iconoclast," Boston published by J. P. Mendum, 1877.

[v] Taken from, <u>Seneca. Epistles, Volume II: Epistles 66-92</u>. Translated by Richard M. Gummere. Loeb Classical Library 76. Cambridge, MA: Harvard University Press, 1920.

[vi] Taken from, <u>Saint Augustine, Translated by Ludwig Schopp, The Fathers of the Church: A New Translation</u> (Patristic series), Vol. 5: Washington: CUA Press, 1948. Used by permission.

[vii] Taken from, <u>Ethics</u> by John Dewey & James H. Tufts. New York: Henry Holt and Company London: George Bell and Sons, 1909.

[viii]Taken from, <u>The Ethics of Confucius. The Sayings of the Master and His Disciples Upon The Conduct Of "The Superior Man"</u>, arranged according to the plan of Confucius with running commentary by Miles Menander Dawson, with a foreword by Wu Ting Fang. New York: G.P. Putnam's Sons, 1915.

[ix] Copyright 2017 by John C. Wilhelmsson. Used by permission.

[x] This translation of Summa Theologica translated by Fathers of the English Dominican Province.

[xi] Taken from, <u>Fundamental Principles Of The Metaphysic Of Morals</u> by Immanuel Kant, 1785. Translated by Thomas Kingsmill Abbott in 1895.

[xii] Taken from, <u>Utilitarianism</u> by John Stuart Mill. Reprinted From 'Fraser's Magazine' Seventh Edition. London: Longmans, Green, And Co., 1879.

[xiii] Copyright 2009 by Rita Manning. Used by permission.